# So This Is Christmas Quiz Book

First published in the UK in 2022 by Studio Press Books,
an imprint of Bonnier Books UK,
4th Floor, Victoria House, Bloomsbury Square, London WC1B 4DA
Owned by Bonnier Books,
Sveavägen 56, Stockholm, Sweden

bonnierbooks.co.uk

3 5 7 9 10 8 6 4 2

ISBN 978-1-80078-339-3

Written by Roland Hall
Edited by Ellie Rose
Designed by Maddox Philpot
Production by Emma Kidd

A CIP catalogue for this book is available from the British Library
Printed and bound in Great Britain by Clays Ltd, Elcograf S.p.A.

# So This Is Christmas Quiz Book

**OVER 1,500 QUESTIONS TO TEST YOUR FESTIVE KNOWLEDGE!**

STUDIO PRESS

# Contents

Introduction                                     6

Quiz 1: General Knowledge                        8

Quiz 2: Christmas TV                            14

Quiz 3: Christmas Number Ones                   20

Quiz 4: Christmas Carols                        26

Quiz 5: Christmas Movies                        32

Quiz 6: Christmas Adverts                       38

Quiz 7: General Knowledge                       44

Quiz 8: Christmas Toys                          50

Quiz 9: *Top of the Pops* Christmas
      Specials     56

Quiz 10: Christmas Celebrations                 62

Quiz 11: Father Christmas                       68

Quiz 12: Christmas Books                        74

Quiz 13: General Knowledge                      80

Quiz 14: Christmas Around
      the World    86

Quiz 15: Christmas Drinks                       92

Quiz 16: Festive Feasts                         98

Quiz 17: Christmas Decoration                  104

Quiz 18: Christmas Trivia            110
Quiz 19: General Knowledge           116
Quiz 20: Christmas Animations        122
Quiz 21: Christmas Songs             128
Quiz 22: Christmas Traditions        134
Quiz 23: Nativity                    140
Quiz 24: Christmas Sport             146
Quiz 25: General Knowledge           152
Quiz 26: Christmas Sweets            158
Quiz 27: Christmas Characters        164
Quiz 28: Christmas Mix               170
Quiz 29: Christmas in the
          British Isles              176
Quiz 30: Yuletide                    182
Quiz 31: General Knowledge           188
Quiz 32: Movie Favourites            194
Quiz 33: Tick Tock                   200
Quiz 34: Happy New Year              206
Answers                              212
Notes                                314

# Introduction

In the festive favourite movie *Love Actually*, there's a song, 'Christmas Is All Around', and it's true. Christmas itself may only be a couple of days spent with loved (and perhaps not-so-loved) ones, but the season goes on for months and seems to get longer every year!

And what months they are – spent with our families and friends, eating lovely food, drinking delicious drinks, present buying, wrapping, giving and receiving, watching favourite movies old and new, singing carols and Christmas hits... The list is endless and it's almost impossible to resist the festive cheer.

Children love Christmas for the sprouts they get to eat, the time they get to spend with Aunty Doris and maybe – just maybe – the odd present or two. Adults love Christmas for the time off work, the hours spent with their nearest and dearest, and maybe – just maybe – the opportunity to spend time eating and drinking as much as they like.

There is so much to Christmas: the traditions, the books, the history, the movies, the carols, the decorations, the food... This book is crammed full of questions on all aspects of the festive season, from sprouts to Santa, Christmas carols to *A Christmas Carol* and 'Last Christmas' (the song) to, well, *Last Christmas* (the movie)!

Just like Christmas and the many celebrations surrounding it, this book has something for everyone. There are 34 quizzes on all manner of topics and each quiz is split into three levels that are ranked in difficulty: One Snowflake (easy), Two Snowflakes (medium) and Three Snowflakes (difficult).

One Snowflake quizzes are suitable for everyone, children and adults alike. Two Snowflake quizzes are a bit more difficult and should provide a challenge for most. Three Snowflake quizzes should have Father Christmas calling the Three Wise Men for help!

So put on your Santa hats, pop some mince pies on the table, pour the mulled wine and settle down for a friendly (or not so friendly) family challenge to see who really knows the true meaning of Christmas!

# General Knowledge

1.  **True or false?** December 25 is known as Christmas Day.

2.  What special songs are usually sung at Christmas?
    a   Carols
    b   Yulesongs
    c   Santas
    d   Classics

3.  **Fill in the blank:** Father Christmas is also known as Santa _____ .

4.  In the UK, Christmas presents are usually exchanged on what day?

5.  What guided the Three Wise Men to Bethlehem?

6.  What is the day after Christmas Day called?

7.  Which British royal makes a speech that is broadcast around the world on Christmas Day?

8.  What did the Herald Angels do in the song?

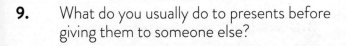

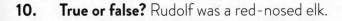

**9.** What do you usually do to presents before giving them to someone else?

**10.** **True or false?** Rudolf was a red-nosed elk.

**11.** **Fill in the blank:** Complete the film title, *The _____ Before Christmas*

**12.** What is the most common Christmas meal in the UK?
  **a** Fish and chips
  **b** Curry
  **c** Cold turkey sandwiches
  **d** Roast turkey

**13.** How many days of Christmas are there in the famous song?

**14.** What comes out of a cracker and can be worn on your head?

**15.** What do you traditionally do under the mistletoe at Christmas?

# Quiz 1

## General Knowledge

1.  **True or false?** Banks are always closed on Christmas Day.

2.  People who sing Christmas songs outside your house, usually for charity, are known as what?
    a   Carol singers
    b   Christmastiders
    c   Timewasters
    d   Wassailers

3.  Father Christmas is also known as Saint what?

4.  **Fill in the blank:** 'We wish you a merry Christmas and a _____ _____ _____ '.

5.  According to the Bible, which precious metal was given to the baby Jesus?

6.  **True or false?** Boxing Day is a day of boxing matches around the world.

7.  Churchgoers often attend a special service on Christmas Eve. What is it called?
    a   Eton Mess
    b   Midnight Confession
    c   Midnight Mass
    d   Midnight Mess

8.  **Fill in the blank:** Complete the Christmas carol title, 'God Rest Ye Merry, _____ '.

**9.** Which tradition were the Victorians responsible for starting?
   **a** Sending puddings
   **b** Sending presents
   **c** Sending cards
   **d** Sending cabbages

**10.** Which of Santa's reindeer shares a name with a female fox?

**11.** What hugely popular kids Christmas movie franchise stretched to six films?

**12.** **True or false?** Australia traditionally gifts a Christmas tree that is displayed in Trafalgar Square, London.

**13.** What did LadBaby love at Christmas in 2019?

**14.** Alongside a paper crown and a toy, what do you usually find in a cracker?
   **a** A joke
   **b** A coded message
   **c** A lottery scratch card
   **d** A recipe

**15.** According to the song, who did I see Mommy kissing under the mistletoe?

Answers on page 213

# General Knowledge

**1.** Which of these German treats is traditionally made with honey; lebkuchen or stollen?

**2.** Carol singing is similar to which old tradition?

**3.** According to tradition, in which European territory does Father Christmas live?

**4.** What type of sauce accompanies turkey, particularly in the USA?

**5.** What are widely regarded as the names of the Three Wise Men who visited Jesus?

**6.** Which of the following has NOT had at least three consecutive Christmas number ones?
**a** LadBaby
**b** The Spice Girls
**c** The Beatles
**d** Wham!

**7.** Where did Mary and Joseph travel from before they reached Bethlehem?

**8.** In the carol, which king looked out on the feast of Stephen?

**9.** In most of continental Europe, Christmas presents are exchanged on what day?

**10.** What popular Christmas song was the first song to be broadcast from space in 1965?

**11.** In the movie *The Expendables*, who plays the character named Lee Christmas?

**12.** Which London street is traditionally the first in the UK to switch on its Christmas lights?

**13.** In what year was 'There's No One Quite Like Grandma' the Christmas number one?

**14.** Which Christmas song has been recorded the most times?

**15.** What was the most desired games console for Christmas 2006?

# Quiz 2

## Christmas TV

**1.** Which book by Raymond Briggs was adapted to become a TV favourite in the 1980s?
   **a** *Father Christmas*
   **b** *The Snowman*
   **c** *The Snow Yeti*
   **d** *The Snow Pig*

**2.** What is the fourth word of 'Jingle Bells'?

**3.** Who is green, grumpy and 'stole Christmas'?

**4.** **True or false?** *Horrid Henry* has had more than one Christmas special on TV.

**5.** **Fill in the blank:** Complete the name of the movie in which two people swap roles and find love, *The _____ Switch*.

**6.** Which is the famous TV snowman?
   **a** Drippy
   **b** Freezy
   **c** Frosty
   **d** Icy

**7.** **Fill in the blank:** Complete the title of this classic poem and TV special, *'Twas the Night Before _____* .

**8.** Which adult talent show had a kids' special in December 2021?

**9.** What sort of Christmas did Postman Pat have in his 2004 TV special?
   **a** Crazy
   **b** Magic
   **c** Sleepy
   **d** Wild

**10.** Which story of a mouse and a monster in a deep, dark wood became a Christmas favourite?

**11.** **True or false?** Terry Pratchett's *The Abominable Snow Baby* was broadcast on TV in 2021.

**12.** Whose Christmas special was called 'The Flight Before Christmas'?

**13.** In *Robin Robin*, what family of animals has raised Robin?

**14.** Who dresses up as Santa in the *Spongebob Squarepants* episode 'Christmas Who'?
   **a** Squidward
   **b** Patrick
   **c** Sandy
   **d** Mr Krabs

**15.** Which TV family has a cat called Snowball?

# Christmas TV

1. In what year was the first *Doctor Who* Christmas special broadcast?

2. What was strange about the Christmas episode of *The Story of Tracy Beaker*?
   a Tracy Beaker wasn't in it
   b It wasn't about Christmas
   c It was a cartoon
   d It was broadcast in February

3. Which band had a 'Party' for their Christmas special in 2008?

4. What famous dogs and cats home has a Christmas special fronted by Paul O'Grady?

5. What was the name of the first *Only Fools and Horses* Christmas special?
   a 'Christmas Joy'
   b 'Christmas Spirit'
   c 'Christmas Crackers'
   d 'Christmas Booze-up'

6. **True or false?** The *Mr Bean* Christmas special was entitled 'We Wish You A Beany Christmas'.

7. **Fill in the blank:** Complete the episode title, 'Simpsons _____ On An Open Fire'.

8. 'Blackadder's Christmas Carol' is based on what famous book?

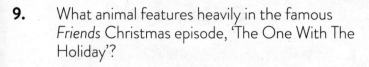

**9.** What animal features heavily in the famous *Friends* Christmas episode, 'The One With The Holiday'?

**10.** **True or false?** Fletcher escapes temporarily in the *Porridge* special 'No Way Out'.

**11.** What was the name of the 2005 *Alan Partridge* Christmas special?

**12.** What was the 2010 *Peep Show* Christmas special called?
   **a** 'Christmas Meetings'
   **b** 'Seasonal Greetings'
   **c** 'Seasonal Beatings'
   **d** 'Christmas Peepings'

**13.** In what year was the first *Strictly Come Dancing* Christmas special?

**14.** What did Abi and Lauren fall off in the *Eastenders* Christmas special in 2017?

**15.** What, according to a BritBox survey, was the UK's favourite Christmas TV moment?
   **a** Stacy tells Gavin she is pregnant (*Gavin and Stacy*)
   **b** Geraldine eats four Christmas lunches (*The Vicar of Dibley*)
   **c** Jim Royle crying when Denise gives birth (*The Royle Family*)
   **d** Del Boy and Rodders dressed up as Batman and Robin (*Only Fools and Horses*)

Answers on page 216

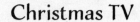

# Quiz 2

## Christmas TV

**1.** In what year did Morecambe and Wise have a Christmas special that featured 'There Is Nothing Like A Dame'?

**2.** In *South Park*, Mr Hankey is a Christmas what?

**3.** Who was *Doctor Who*'s enemy in the 2012 Christmas special?

**4.** What long-running American series began with the TV movie, *The Homecoming: A Christmas Story*?

**5.** Which puppet show had a Christmas special broadcast on BritBox in 2021?

**6.** Which famous series concluded with a two-part Christmas special in 2003?

**7.** What was the name of the first Christmas special episode of *The West Wing*?

**8.** What type of dog is Santa's Little Helper in *The Simpsons*?

**9.** What show had an episode named 'The Constant'?

**10.** In *Six Feet Under*, on what day does Nathaniel Fisher die?

**11.** At the end of the 1999 Christmas special of *The Royle Family*, what happens to Denise?

**12.** What is the name of the *Bottom* Christmas special?

**13.** How many Christmas trees do the Belcher family buy in the *Bob's Burgers* episode, 'Christmas in the Car'?

**14.** What was the title of the *Scrubs* Christmas episode in season one?

**15.** What year was the *Men Behaving Badly* Christmas special first broadcast?

# Quiz 3

## Christmas Number Ones

**1.** Who had four consecutive Christmas number ones, from 2018 to 2021?

**2.** What was the title of the Band Aid song from 1984?

**3.** **Fill in the blank:** Harry Belafonte's Christmas hit, 'Mary's Boy _____ .'

**4.** What band sang 'Killing in the Name' when it topped the Christmas chart in 2009?

**5.** **True or false?** Mr Blobby's famous song was called 'Mr Blobby'.

**6.** Girls Aloud hit number one in 2002 with which song?
   **a** 'Going Underground'
   **b** 'Santa Underground'
   **c** 'Sound of the Underground'
   **d** 'Underground Overground'

**7.** **True or false?** Bob the Builder has had a Christmas number one in the UK.

**8.** Who were the two guest singers on LadBaby's 2021 Christmas chart-topper?

**9.** Who sang with Gareth Malone on the song 'Wherever You Are'?

**10.** Whose 'Earth Song' was a Christmas number one in 1995?

**11.** **Fill in the blank:** The title of the 2012 song from the Justice Collective, 'He Ain't Heavy, He's My _____'.

**12.** **True or false?** Band Aid and Band Aid 20 had a Christmas number one with the same song.

**13.** What was Benny Hill's Christmas number one called?
   **a** 'Benny (The Fastest Comedian in London)'
   **b** 'Bert (The Fastest Milkman in the West)'
   **c** 'Ernie (The Fastest Milkman in the West)'
   **d** 'The Benny Hill Theme Tune'

**14.** Who sang 'Rockabye'?

**15.** What food was mentioned in the title of two of LadBaby's Christmas number ones?

# Quiz 3

## Christmas Number Ones

1. Which band sang 'Mull of Kintyre'?

2. **Fill in the blank:** Complete the title of the 1988 song, 'Mistletoe and _____'.

3. What colour was the 'Grass of Home' that Tom Jones sang about?

4. Which of these was NOT a Christmas number one for the Beatles?
   a 'Day Tripper'/'We Can Work It Out'
   b 'Eleanor Rigby'
   c 'I Feel Fine'
   d 'I Want to Hold Your Hand'

5. Where was Jimmy Osmond's 'Long Haired Lover' from?

6. To whom did Slade wish a Merry Christmas?

7. Who was 'Perfect' with a Christmas number one in 2017?

8. What were the names of all three of the Spice Girls's Christmas number ones between 1996–1998?

9. What was the title of Alexandra Burke's 2008 Christmas number one?

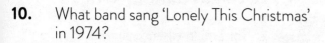

**10.** What band sang 'Lonely This Christmas' in 1974?

**11. True or false?** Pink Floyd had a Christmas number one with 'Money'.

**12.** Who did Robbie Williams duet with in 2001 to reach the top of the Christmas chart?

**13.** What was the title of Matt Cardle's 2010 Christmas chart-topper?

**14.** What song did the Lewisham and Greenwich NHS Choir sing in 2015?

**15.** What kind of world did Michael Andrews and Gary Jules sing about in 2003?
   **a** Sad
   **b** Bad
   **c** Mad
   **d** Fad

Answers on page 219

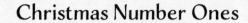

# Quiz 3

## Christmas Number Ones

**1.** Queen's 'Bohemian Rhapsody' was the Christmas number one in 1991. It was a double-A release; what was the other song?

**2.** What was the name of the melody the song 'When A Child is Born' is based on?

**3.** What was the Beatles' final Christmas number one?

**4.** In what year was Elvis Presley the Christmas number one with 'Return to Sender'?

**5.** According to the Official Charts, what year was the first Christmas number one in the UK?

**6.** What is the full title of Boney M.'s 1978 Christmas number one?

**7.** What is the only song that has twice been a Christmas number one for the same artist?

**8.** Who has the record for most consecutive Christmas number ones?

**9.** What was the title of Sam Bailey's Christmas number one?

**10.** How many times has Cliff Richard featured in a Christmas number one?

**11.** What is the only band to have a Christmas number one and number two at the same time?

**12.** Which day of the week was the 2015 Christmas number one revealed?

**13.** What is the biggest selling Christmas number one of all time?

**14.** What charity is the main beneficiary of LadBaby's songs?

**15.** What is the name of Danny Williams' 1961 chart-topping Christmas hit?

# Quiz 4

## Christmas Carols

1. How many kings are there in the famous carol?

2. What do they 'Deck the Halls' with?

3. On the first day of Christmas, what did my true love send to me?

4. **True or false?** There is a Christmas song called 'We Wish You A Smelly Christmas'.

5. **Fill in the blank:** Complete the name of the carol, '_____ _____ Merrily On High'.

6. What goes with holly in the title of a famous carol?

7. Who is asleep in 'Away In A Manger'?

8. What did Good King Wenceslas look out on?

9. What is the 'little town' in the title of the famous carol?

10. **Fill in the blank:** Complete the song title, 'Silent _____ '.

11. **True or false?** There is a famous carol called 'The Last Noel'.

**12.** What did shepherds do by night, according to the title of the carol?

**13.** Which carol is about a Christmas tree?
   **a** 'Have A Tree-mendous Christmas'
   **b** 'My Lovely Tree'
   **c** 'Lovely Log'
   **d** 'O Tannenbaum'

**14.** **Fill in the blank:** Complete the song title, 'O Come All Yve _____ '.

**15.** According to the 2021 poll, what is the UK's favourite Christmas carol?
   **a** 'Hark! The Herald Angels Sing'
   **b** 'O Come All Ye Faithful'
   **c** 'Away In A Manger'
   **d** 'O Holy Night'

Answers on page 221

# Quiz 4

## Christmas Carols

1. Where was 'O Little Town of Bethlehem' written: Germany, the UK or the USA?

2. Who wrote 'In the Bleak Midwinter'?

3. What carol is sung outside Scrooge's office in *A Christmas Carol*?

4. **Fill in the blank:** Complete the song title, 'Joy to the _____ '.

5. Which carol was previously known as 'Carol of the Drum'?

6. In the song, what sort of road was the 'Little Donkey' walking on?

7. **Fill in the blank:** A Christmas song by Bing Crosby and David Bowie was called '_____ _____ _____ / Little Drummer Boy'.

8. **True or false?** 'Do You Hear What I Hear' was written in the 16th century.

9. In what year was carol singing banned in England: 1647, 1747 or 1847?

10. From which country did 'Deck the Halls' originate?

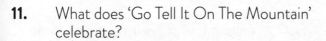

**11.** What does 'Go Tell It On The Mountain' celebrate?

**12.** **True or false?** 'Silent Night' was originally written in German.

**13.** **Fill in the blank:** Complete the song title, 'See Amid the Winter's _____ '.

**14.** In 'Away in a Manger', the baby had no what for a bed?

**15.** **Fill in the blank:** Complete the song title, 'It Came Upon A _____ Clear'.

## Christmas Carols

**1.** 'For Unto Us A Child is Born' is from which famous piece of music?

**2.** Franz Xaver Gruber and Father Joseph Mohr wrote which famous carol?

**3.** In what language were the original lyrics to 'O Come, O Come, Emmanuel'?

**4.** Who wrote the lyrics to 'Hark! The Herald Angels Sing'?

**5.** What stood in 'Royal David's City'?

**6.** What does *In Dulci Jubilo* mean literally?

**7.** Where did the ships sail to in 'I Saw Three Ships'?

**8.** 'Lully lulla' are the opening words of which carol?

**9.** What is the total number of gifts given in 'The Twelve Days of Christmas'?

**10.** What do the singers demand to be brought to them in 'We Wish You A Merry Christmas'?

**11.** What is thought to be the first Christmas song to mention Santa Claus?

**12.** Who was the real King Wenceslas?

**13.** What was the gift on the third day of Christmas?

**14.** Who wrote the poem that 'Once In Royal David's City' is based on?

**15.** In what year was the first acknowledged carol service in England?

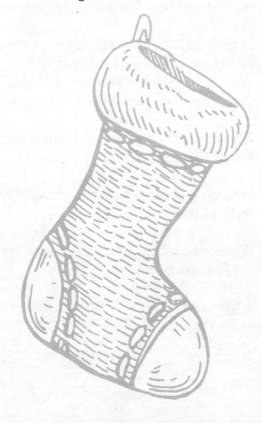

# Christmas Movies

**1.** In *Elf*, who raised Buddy?

**2.** **Fill in the blank:** Complete the movie title, *Jingle Jangle: A _____ Journey*.

**3.** Whose place does Scott Calvin have to take in *The Santa Clause*?

**4.** When Kevin first wakes up in *Home Alone*, how many people are in the house with him?

**5.** *Scrooged* is a modern take on what story?

**6.** What is the name of Mackenzie Walsh's godmother in *Godmothered*?

**7.** In what county do the Claus family end up in *Arthur Christmas*: Cornwall or Essex?

**8.** Who do Teddy and Kate find in their living room in *The Christmas Chronicles*?

**9.** What fictional country is the setting for *The Princess Switch*?

**10.** Which actor plays the narrator and conductor in *The Polar Express*?

**11.** In which of the following Harry Potter films does Harry spend Christmas at Hogwarts?
  **a** *Harry Potter and the Christmas Party at Hogwarts*
  **b** *Harry Potter and the Order of the Phoenix*
  **c** *Harry Potter and the Goblet of Fire*
  **d** *Harry Potter and the Philosopher's Stone*

**12.** Which Christmas animated movie features the song 'Walking in the Air'?

**13.** **Fill in the blank:** Complete the movie title, *Edward _____* .

**14.** What is the name of the prince in *A Christmas Prince*?

**15.** Which actor is the star of *Jingle All the Way*?

# Christmas Movies

**1.** Which Christmas movie, starring James Stewart and Donna Reed, often tops the charts of most popular Christmas film ever?

**2.** What movie was the first to feature the song 'White Christmas' by Bing Crosby?

**3.** On which street is there a famous movie miracle?
**a** Oxford
**b** 82nd
**c** Gower
**d** 34th

**4.** Which actor is the star of *Meet Me In St Louis*?

**5.** At which airport does John McClane arrive in *Die Hard*?

**6.** Who is the central character in *The Man Who Invented Christmas*?

**7.** Billy Bob Thornton played Willie T. Stokes in which grown-up Christmas classic?

**8.** Who plays Ebeneezer Scrooge in *The Muppet Christmas Carol*?

**9.** What is the name of Bill Nighy's character in *Love Actually*?

**10.** What comedy duo were the stars of the 1934 movie *Babes in Toyland*?

**11.** Who plays Bridget Jones in *Bridget Jones's Diary*?

**12.** Who plays Matthew Broderick's new neighbour in *Deck the Halls*?

**13.** What is the full name of the movie, *The Family...*
   **a** *Affair*
   **b** *Christmas*
   **c** *Rock*
   **d** *Stone*

**14.** Who directed the 2000 movie *How the Grinch Stole Christmas*?

**15.** As of 2022, how many movies are there in the *Home Alone* series?

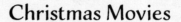

# Quiz 5

## Christmas Movies

**1.** What is the name of the Harold and Kumar Christmas movie?

**2.** In *Batman Returns*, what is The Penguin's real name?

**3.** In the 2021 movie *Silent Night*, who is hosting the Christmas dinner?

**4.** Who plays Jude Law's love interest in *The Holiday*?

**5.** *White Christmas* follows a similar storyline to which classic movie?

**6.** What is the name of Chevy Chase's character in *National Lampoon's Christmas Vacation*?

**7.** What must you NEVER do with a mogwai?

**8.** Who starred in *The Man in the Santa Claus Suit*?

**9.** What 2019 movie paired Emilia Clarke and Emma Thompson as mother and daughter?

**10.** What is the name of the company that is central to *Office Christmas Party*?

**11.** Who does Sandra Bullock's character work for in *While You Were Sleeping*?

**12.** Which classic Christmas song features in
*Meet Me In St Louis*?

**13.** Who directed *It's A Wonderful Life*?

**14.** What is the name of Seth Rogen's character in
*The Night Before*?

**15.** Who played the part of Kris Kringle in the 1947
movie *Miracle on 34th Street*?

Answers on page 226

# Christmas Adverts

**1.** John Lewis and Waitrose's 2021 Christmas advertisement featured a boy and what other creature?

**2.** Which vegetable was the star of Aldi's 2021 Christmas advert?
   **a** Aubergine
   **b** Carrot
   **c** Potato
   **d** Pumpkin

**3.** In the 2021 Coca-Cola Christmas advert, what do the residents make for their building?

**4.** What song plays in the 2021 Lidl Christmas advert?

**5.** Who was the star of the Marks & Spencer Christmas advert in 2021?

**6.** What kind of dad stars in the 2021 Disney Christmas advert?

**7.** In Asda's 2021 Christmas advert, what are (most) people wearing on their feet?

**8.** What is the dog playing on in the classic John Lewis Christmas ad from 2016?

**9.** What was the tagline of the 2021 Argos advert?
   **a** Christmas is On
   **b** Christmas Rocks
   **c** Christmas is Off
   **d** Christmas is Great

**10.** What song has accompanied the Quality Street advertisements for years?

**11.** The John Lewis Christmas ad of 2015 featured the man on the what?

**12.** Sainsbury's made a famous advert with the Royal British Legion in 2014. In what year was it set?

**13.** Whose eternally famous Christmas ad from 1992 featured a boy who wasn't tall enough and some mistletoe?

**14.** What supermarket made an advert featuring Nicholas the Sweep?

**15.** **True or false?** Jamie Oliver was the star of the John Lewis Christmas ad in 2018.

Answers on page 227

# Christmas Adverts

1. Which product featured the line, 'Mummy made the gravy'?

2. Which store's now-classic 1983 advert was a 'Spectacular Christmas Show'?

3. John Lewis's 2011 advert featured an impatient boy. What does he do at the end?

4. According to the advert, Old Spice was the what of a man?
   a Making
   b Mark
   c Smell
   d Whiff

5. What sort of animal was Monty, from the 2014 John Lewis Christmas ad?

6. What did the children leave out for Santa in the 1991 Kellogg's ad?

7. What vehicle features heavily in Coca-Cola Christmas advertising?

8. What shop's Christmas ad campaign was based around the saying, 'This is not just...'?

9. What fizzy drink advert featured a tongue-in-cheek version of *The Snowman*?

**10.** Which shop's 2014 ad featured a tired NHS worker coming home after a late shift?

**11.** Who sang 'Somewhere Only We Know' in the 2013 John Lewis Christmas ad?

**12.** John Lewis's Christmas advert from 2012 featured a couple of loving what?
  **a** Cats
  **b** Dogs
  **c** Carrots
  **d** Snowpeople

**13.** Whose 2021 Christmas ad featured a boy in shiny boots playing an organ in a village hall?

**14.** Which sports store's 2021 Christmas ad featured an extended street scene in Manchester?

**15.** Which store had an advert featuring a never-ending bag of presents?

# Quiz 6

## Christmas Adverts

1. Which company's 2021 Christmas advert featured a bird feeder at the end?

2. Whose 2021 Christmas advert started with the words, 'Welcome to the house of festive'?

3. Which department store's 2021 Christmas advert was called 'Christmas of Dreams'?

4. Which shop invited you to 'Go All Out' at Christmas 2021?

5. A little yellow man fronted Christmas ads for which product throughout the 1990s?

6. The Argos Christmas advert from 2012 featured a whole family of what?

7. In 2016 Marks & Spencer's Christmas ad featured who making a delivery by helicopter?

8. Aldi have featured a carrot in their Christmas adverts for a number of years. What is its name?

9. Which supermarket's 2018 Christmas advert took place at a primary school concert?

10. What company claimed to be 'Reindeer ready' in 2019?

**11.** Which company's 2020 Christmas ad had the tagline 'From Our Family To Yours'?

**12.** Who directed Coca-Cola's famous 2020 epic Christmas advert?

**13.** What bird starred in Waitrose's 2016 Christmas advert?

**14.** What creatures feature in the famous Heathrow Airport Christmas ads?

**15.** Who directed H&M's famous 2016 Christmas advert that starred Adrien Brody?

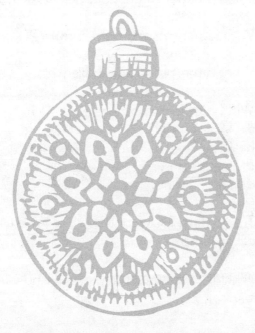

## General Knowledge

**1.** What is the first sequel to *A Christmas Prince* called?

**2.** **True or false?** The Rubik's Cube was the number one Christmas toy in 2020.

**3.** What is usually the last day to open on an advent calendar?

**4.** What do you leave empty for Santa to fill on Christmas Eve?

**5.** **Fill in the blank:** Complete the title of the Christmas pantomime, 'Jack and the _____'.

**6.** Who famously said, 'Bah! Humbug!'

**7.** What is the 'pig' in pigs in blankets?

**8.** What is glühwein?
   **a** Fizzy wine
   **b** Glue
   **c** Ice cream
   **d** Mulled wine

**9.** **True or false?** One of the Three Wise Men was called Caspar.

**10.** What is the name of the sequel to *The Santa Clause*?

11. **Fill the blank:** Name the famous pantomime dame, Mother _____ .

12. Is Yorkshire Pudding sweet or savoury?

13. **True or false?** Every snowflake is unique.

14. In the *Harry Potter* series, how many Christmas trees were put up in the Great Hall at Hogwarts?

15. Who is *petit papa noël*?

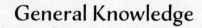

# Quiz 7

## General Knowledge

1. What song spent five weeks at number two in the UK charts at Christmas in 1984?

2. What nationality is José Feliciano, singer of 'Feliz Navidad'?

3. In 2021, what was the second most viewed programme on TV at Christmas in England?

4. **True or false?** On Channel 4, Rory Bremner, once broadcast an alternative Christmas Message dressed as the Queen.

5. In *Love Actually*, what does the song 'Love Is All Around' become?

6. What band was kept off the top spot at Christmas in 1993 by Mr Blobby, landing the number two spot?

7. In *A Christmas Story*, what does Flick get stuck to the flagpole?

8. In Ukraine, who is known as *Svyatyi Mykolai*?

9. What, traditionally, is placed in the window on Christmas Eve in Ireland?

10. What was gifted to the USA from France in 1886?

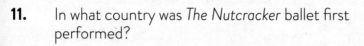

**11.** In what country was *The Nutcracker* ballet first performed?

**12.** The word Christmas comes from *Christes maesse*, what does it mean?

**13.** On what day do the events of *The Polar Express* begin?

**14.** How long did it take Judy the Elf to perfect the hot cocoa she makes in *The Santa Clause*?

**15.** What colour is the sash worn by the person who symbolises Santa Lucia in Sweden?

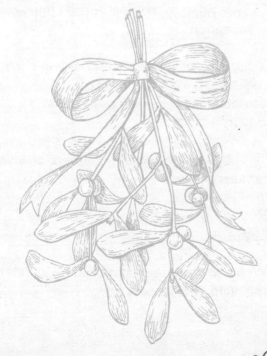

# General Knowledge

**1.** In which New York store did Mariah Carey and Justin Bieber film their video for 'All I Want For Christmas Is You'?

**2.** When was Christmas reinstated as a holiday after it was banned in England?

**3.** 'Last Christmas' by Wham! was a double-A side. What was the other song?

**4.** In what year was the first official Christmas card sent in England?

**5.** On what date is the Feast of the Immaculate Conception?

**6.** What is *bakalar*, a Christmas dish in Croatia?

**7.** On what day is Christmas celebrated in Egypt?

**8.** Tipsy Laird is a Scottish equivalent of which famous dessert?

**9.** By what name is the song 'Adeste Fideles' better known?

**10.** Who delivers presents to children in Italy on the night of 5 January?

**11.** Why does Norway gift a Christmas Tree to the UK every year for display in Trafalgar Square?

**12.** What is the most traditional shape for a Mexican Christmas piñata?

**13.** What does *Nollaig Shona Dhuit* mean in English?

**14.** *Pōhutukawa* is a special Christmas tree in which country?

**15.** Who played the part of Clarence in *It's A Wonderful Life*?

# Quiz 8

## Christmas Toys

1. What is the name of the little animal families and their houses that first became a huge hit in 1987?

2. In 1988 the movie Batman hit the cinemas. What related vehicle was a top Christmas toy?

3. **True or false?** GameBoy was a colour console.

4. Which is the odd one out?
   a Red Ranger
   b Black Ranger
   c Pink Ranger
   d Orange Ranger

5. **Fill in the blank:** Buzz Lightyear's catchphrase is, 'To infinity and _____ '.

6. **True or false?** One of the original Teletubbies was called PooPoo.

7. **Fill in the blank:** Bob the Builder's catchphrase is, 'Can we fix it? _____ _____ _____ !'.

8. In 2005, Microsoft launched a new version of their games console. What was it called?

9. What consumer electronics giant made the Wii games console?

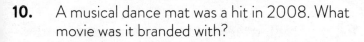

**10.** A musical dance mat was a hit in 2008. What movie was it branded with?

**11.** Leapfrog made an educational tablet in 2011 that was a bestseller. What was it called?
   **a** FrogPad
   **b** LeapPad
   **c** LiftOff
   **d** PondPad

**12.** After the release of *Star Wars: The Force Awakens* in 2015, a new range of toys was available. What colour was Kylo Ren's lightsaber?

**13.** Elsa and Anna dolls were hot toys in 2013; which chilly movie did they star in?

**14.** The Smurfs first aired in 1981, but what colour are they?

**15.** **True or false?** A BMX is a type of scooter.

## Christmas Toys

**1.** In 1988 what would you hope to 'catch' with your Proton Pack?

**2.** **Fill in the blank:** Shredder was a villain and popular action figure from *Teenage Mutant* _____ _____ .

**3.** Which island was a bestseller for *Thunderbirds* in 1992?

**4.** What was the name of the 'milk caps' that became a huge collectible success?

**5.** What was the bestselling boardgame of 1999 related to a very popular TV show?

**6.** Which dolls had a 'passion for fashion' in 2002?

**7.** Spinning tops made a comeback in 2002; what were these futuristic versions called?

**8.** What was the name of Sony's handheld games console?

**9.** **True or false?** Mr Squiggles was a battery powered plush mouse GoGo Pet.

**10.** In 2010 which *Toy Story* movie was a bestseller on DVD?
 **a** *Toy Story*
 **b** *Toy Story 2*
 **c** *Toy Story 3*
 **d** *Toy Story 4*

**11.** Which movie's toy collection was a hit in 1977?

**12.** Simon was an electronic game with four colour panels. Which of these was NOT a colour:
 **a** Blue
 **b** Green
 **c** Purple
 **d** Yellow

**13.** **True or false?** The Rubik's Cube was invented by Ernő Rubik.

**14.** What Patch Kid was popular in 1983?

**15.** Transformers toys became bestsellers after the series debuted in 1984; what were the villains known as?

Answers on page 234

# Quiz 8

## Christmas Toys

**1.** Which Transformer was the must-have toy for Christmas 1985?

**2.** What bestseller from 1986 prompted the saying 'got, got, need'?

**3.** What sort of pet was a Tamagotchi?

**4.** In what year was Furby launched?

**5.** What was the name of the robotic dog that was a huge hit in 2000?

**6.** What does Igglepiggle have in their hand?

**7.** In what year did *Skylanders* first hit the shops?

**8.** Furby made a comeback in 2013; what was the little creature called?

**9.** Who made the 2600 games console?

**10.** Which of these is not a real Care Bear?
   **a** Cheer Bear
   **b** Funshine Bear
   **c** Grumpy Bear
   **d** Wuvvy Bear

**11.** What was the name of the 'ball' that was a hit at Christmas in 1987?

**12.** The NES was a huge-selling electronic games console; what do the letters stand for?

**13.** What sort of 'babies' were a huge hit from the mid-1990s?

**14.** If someone says, 'Gotta catch 'em all!', what are they talking about?

**15.** What is the name of the bestselling toy that was made popular by the Disney series *The Mandalorian*?

# Quiz 9

## Top of the Pops Christmas Specials

1. What year was the first *Top of the Pops* Christmas special broadcast?
   a 1864
   b 1919
   c 1964
   d 2004

2. Which famous band held the number one spot in 1964?

3. **Fill in the blank:** Complete the song title, 'I _____ It Could Be Christmas Every Day'.

4. **True or false?** In 1966 the *Top of the Pops* Christmas special was split into seven parts and shown every day over Christmas week.

5. In 1968 The Scaffold had a Christmas hit with 'Lily the...'
   a Blue
   b Pink
   c Red
   d Vermillion

6. What band sang 'Merry Xmas Everybody'?

7. **Fill in the blank:** The 1969 *Top of the Pops* Christmas special featured 'Bad _____ Rising' by Credence Clearwater Revival.

**8.** On which day were the *Top of the Pops* Christmas specials NOT commonly broadcast?
a Christmas Eve
b Christmas Day
c Boxing Day
d New Year's Eve

**9.** **True or false?** There was no *Top of the Pops* Christmas special broadcast in 2021.

**10.** Which of the following was a regular presenter of *Top of the Pops* Christmas specials in the 2000s?
a Fearne Cotton
b Cat Deeley
c Emma Bunton
d Sharon Osborne

**11.** Which two chart-toppers introduced the *Top of the Pops* Christmas special in 2021?

**12.** What was the name of Ed Sheeran's first Christmas number one?

**13.** What song did Anne-Marie sing on the show in 2021?

**14.** **True or false?** The Christmas special in 2021 featured a new *Top of the Pops* theme tune.

**15.** What did LadBaby eat for their Christmas dinner in 2021?

# *Top of the Pops Christmas Specials*

1.  What song was kept off the number one spot by Band Aid's 'Do They Know It's Christmas?'?

2.  Which two bands released Christmas-themed songs in 1973, with a view to getting the Christmas number one spot?

3.  What anniversary did the Christmas number one celebrate in 2021?
    a  50th
    b  60th
    c  70th
    d  80th

4.  What was the last Christmas number one to feature Christmas in the title?

5.  And what was the last number one to feature Christmas in the title prior to the answer above?

6.  **True or false?** Anne-Marie sings on Clean Bandit's 'Rockabye'.

7.  Who featured on 'I Wish' by Joel Correy?

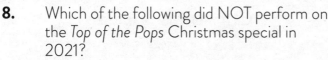

**8.** Which of the following did NOT perform on the *Top of the Pops* Christmas special in 2021?
   **a** BTS
   **b** Tom Grennan
   **c** Griff
   **d** Mimi Webb

**9.** Who released the album *Music of the Spheres* in 2021?

**10.** Who sang 'Home to You (This Christmas)' on the 2021 *Top of the Pops* Christmas special?

**11.** **Fill in the blank:** Complete the song title, 'Little Bit of _____ ' by Tom Grennan.

**12.** Who recorded the song 'I Don't Wanna Talk (I Just Wanna Dance)'?

**13.** What was the bestselling song of 2021 in the UK?

**14.** **Fill in the blank:** Complete the Lil Nas X song title, 'Montero ( _____ _____ _____ _____ _____ )'.

**15.** **True or false?** Olivia Rodrigo had five songs in the top 10 at the same time in 2021.

# Quiz 9

## *Top of the Pops Christmas Specials*

1. In what year did Slade have a Christmas number one with 'Merry Xmas Everybody'?

2. How many years after the song's first release did Rage Against the Machine's 'Killing in the Name' reach the Christmas number one slot?

3. How many Christmas number ones have had the word Christmas or Xmas in the title?

4. Which Irish boyband featured on the *Top of the Pops* Christmas special in 2000?

5. Who sang with Clean Bandit on the *Top of the Pops* Christmas special in 2021?

6. What song links Boney M. and Harry Belafonte?

7. How many times has 'Do They Know It's Christmas' topped the charts, and in which year(s)?

8. **Fill in the blank:** Complete the band name, Sam and the _____ .

9. Which bestselling female artist sang 'I'll Be There For You' on *Top of the Pops* on Christmas Day in 2018?

**10.** Olly Alexander featured on *Top of the Pops* in 2018 under what name?

**11.** Which female presenter was a regular in the 2010s, at first with Fearne Cotton then with other co-hosts?

**12.** What song did DNCE perform on the 2016 special?

**13.** In what year did Sigrid first appear on a *Top of the Pops* Christmas special?

**14.** How many times have Clean Bandit appeared on *Top of the Pops* Christmas specials?

**15.** What song did Adele sing on the 2016 *Top of the Pops* Christmas special?

# Christmas Celebrations

1. **True or false?** At Christmas, people often go to church.

2. What is the term for a play that tells the story of the birth of Jesus?

3. Where do you hang tinsel, baubles and other ornaments at Christmas?

4. Where do people traditionally hang a Christmas wreath?
   a Front door
   b On a Christmas tree
   c Toilet door
   d Under mistletoe

5. **True or false?** Christmas trees are sometimes made of plastic.

6. **Fill in the blank:** Complete the saying, 'Christmas is the season of _____ '.

7. What, traditionally, hangs with holly?

8. What sort of special play is popular in theatres at Christmas?

9. What do carollers do?

**10.** What is the 'blanket' in pigs in blankets?

**11.** How was the Queen's speech broadcast in 1952?
- **a** Radio
- **b** Television
- **c** TikTok
- **d** Town crier

**12.** **True or false?** Mince pies are made with beef mince.

**13.** **True or false?** Nearly one billion Christmas cards are sent in the UK each year.

**14.** Each year companies produce and broadcast on television special Christmas versions of what?

**15.** **True or false?** It is traditional to eat Hot Cross Buns at Christmas.

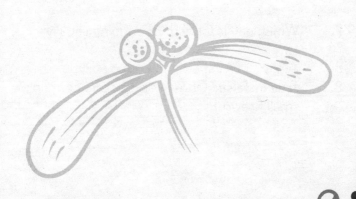

# Quiz 10

## Christmas Celebrations

1. Which ruler of the UK 'cancelled' Christmas in the 17th century?

2. In which century did Christmas trees become widely popular in the UK?
   a  13th
   b  15th
   c  17th
   d  19th

3. **True or false?** There is a plant called the Christmas cactus.

4. What unexpected object brings good luck if you find one in your Christmas pudding?

5. Alongside cream and cocoa, what is the other main ingredient of Bailey's Irish Cream?

6. What was the name of the man who invented Christmas crackers?

7. Which day is Christmas pudding usually eaten?

8. **True or false?** Christmas crackers contain small fireworks.

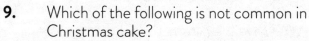

**9.** Which of the following is not common in Christmas cake?
   **a** Brandy
   **b** Marzipan
   **c** Peanuts
   **d** Raisins

**10.** Which of Santa's reindeer has a name that means lightning in German?

**11.** What do you add to champagne to make Buck's Fizz?

**12.** On what day should you take down your Christmas decorations?

**13.** **True or false?** A pantomime dame is usually played by a woman.

**14.** What outdoor place to shop for food and gifts at Christmas is a common import from Europe?

**15.** **True or false?** Mulled wine usually contains no alcohol.

# Christmas Celebrations

**1.** Who gave the Alternative Christmas Message on Channel 4 in 2021?

**2.** In what year did the Post Office stop delivering letters on Christmas Day in England, Wales and Northern Ireland?

**3.** What do you traditionally pour on a Christmas pudding to set it alight?

**4.** What year was the first John Lewis Christmas advert broadcast?

**5.** What is added to butter to make a festive treat for the dinner table?

**6.** Which southern English coastal city has seen a traditional Christmas Day swim since 1860?

**7.** Who was the first British monarch to make a Christmas day broadcast?

**8.** Approximately how many people in the UK watched the Queen's speech in 2021?

**9.** In which Central American country do they perform *La Quema del Diablo*, where an effigy of the devil is placed upon rubbish and then burned?

**10.** According to a YouGov poll, which vegetable is more popular on Christmas dinner plates in the UK, broccoli or sprouts?

**11.** What is commonly found on top of a Christingle?

**12.** How many days after Christmas is Epiphany?

**13.** What are the main ingredients of bread sauce?

**14.** In the USA (and further afield), which plant is commonly associated with Christmas?

**15.** In what year did Boxing Day became a bank holiday in Scotland?

# Quiz 11

## Father Christmas

1. **Fill in the blank:** Complete the name of the song, made famous by Gene Autry, 'Here Comes _____ _____ '.

2. **True or false?** Father Christmas usually stars in a pantomime at Christmas.

3. What does Father Christmas sit in to travel around the world?

4. What animals transport Father Christmas around the world?

5. According to legend, who builds toys for Father Christmas?

6. It is common to meet Father Christmas in the run up to Christmas. Where would you commonly see him?
   a A cabin
   b A cave
   c A den
   d A grotto

7. **True or false?** Father Christmas has a big white beard in most images.

8. How does Father Christmas usually enter a house?

**9.** **True or false?** Saint Rick is a common name for Father Christmas.

**10.** What is the phrase Father Christmas is famous for saying?

**11.** Which of the following is NOT one of Santa's reindeer?
  **a** Blitzen
  **b** Donner
  **c** Prancer
  **d** Spritzer

**12.** Traditionally, who leaves something to eat and drink for Father Christmas: parents or children?

**13.** **True or false?** Father Christmas has a Not-sure List.

**14.** How do children let Father Christmas know what presents they would like?

**15.** We don't know for sure where Father Christmas lives, but which of the following is definitely NOT his residence?
  **a** Alaska
  **b** Barbados
  **c** Lapland
  **d** North Pole

# Quiz 11

## Father Christmas

1.  By what title is the poem 'A Visit from St. Nicholas' more commonly known?

2.  In what year was the famous book about Rudolph the Reindeer first published?

3.  **True or false?** Kris Kringle is another name for Father Christmas.

4.  Where was Clement Clarke Moore born?

5.  What is the name of Father Christmas's wife?

6.  How many reindeer pull Father Christmas's sleigh?

7.  According to tradition, what does Father Christmas deliver if you are on his naughty list?

8.  **True or false?** In Canada, Father Christmas's postcode is POLE 111.

9.  Traditionally, what vegetable should you leave out for Father Christmas's reindeer?

10. What do children in France and Belgium call Father Christmas?

**11.** Why did Father Christmas need Rudolph to lead his sleigh?

**12.** What beverage often features Father Christmas in its Christmas advertising?

**13.** **True or false?** There are multiple towns in the USA called Santa Claus.

**14.** According to the song, how many times does Father Christmas check his list?

**15.** What song about Father Christmas has been recorded to great success since 1934 by the Jackson 5, Mariah Carey, Bruce Springsteen, Michael Bublé (and more)?

Answers on page 243

# Quiz 11

## Father Christmas

1. Saint Nicholas is best known as the patron saint of children and who else?

2. What is the title of the 1977 festive-themed song by Emerson, Lake & Palmer?

3. What organisation famously tracks Father Christmas's sleigh around the world each year?

4. Where is the North Pole theme park, 'the home of Santa's Workshop' which sits at the foot of Pikes Peak?

5. Saint Nicholas is believed to have been a real person, Bishop Nicholas of Myra. What present-day country was he from?

6. In Germany, when saint worship was banned, who replaced Saint Nicholas as the spirit of Christmas?

7. Who wrote "Twas The Night Before Christmas'?

8. In what country is the town of Saint-Nicolas-de-Port, near where Saint Nicholas is believed to have performed a miracle?

9. In Finland there is a real post office called Santa's Post Office. What is the postcode?

**10.** When is Saint Nicholas day?

**11.** Which English band released a single entitled 'Father Christmas' in 1977?

**12.** Which of the following is NOT a real movie featuring Father Christmas:
   **a** *The Man in the Santa Claus Suit*
   **b** *Santa Baby 2: Christmas Maybe*
   **c** *Santa Claus Down Under*
   **d** *The Town Santa Forgot*

**13.** What sort of Santa Claus was a hit song for Mabel Scott in 1948?

**14.** According to the song, what sort of sleigh is 'oh what fun' to ride?

**15.** Who recorded the song 'Santa Baby' in 1953?

# Christmas Books

**1.** What did the Grinch do to Christmas?

**2.** What did J.R.R. Tolkien publish a book of, reputedly written originally by Father Christmas?

**3.** What animal did J.K. Rowling write a Christmas book about?

**4.** What was the title of Julia Donaldson's book about a Christmas tree?

**5.** **Fill in the blank:** Complete the festive book title, *Christmasaurus and the* _____
_____ .

**6.** Whose Christmas book was published over 40 years after the original classic by Shirley Hughes?

**7.** **Fill in the blank:** The famous Christmas train is called The _____ Express.

**8.** How many spirits of Christmas visit Scrooge in *A Christmas Carol*?

**9.** How many pets does Father Christmas have in *Father Christmas* by Raymond Briggs?

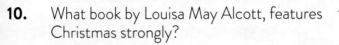

**10.** What book by Louisa May Alcott, features Christmas strongly?

**11.** **True or false?** The Snowman gets around by driving a car.

**12.** What is the correct title of the story by Hans Christian Andersen?
  **a** *The Big Match Girl*
  **b** *The Football Match Girl*
  **c** *The Little Match Girl*
  **d** *The Poor Match Girl*

**13.** **True or false?** LadBaby wrote a book about a sausage roll called Fred.

**14.** **Fill in the blank:** Complete the title of the book series by Matt Haig, *A Boy Called* _____ .

**15.** Which of these is NOT a real Mr Men book?
  **a** *Mr Men A Christmas Carol*
  **b** *Mr Men The Christmas Party*
  **c** *Mr Men Meet Father Christmas*
  **d** *Mr Men and the Christmas Ghosts*

## Christmas Books

**1.** What did Father Christmas do in Raymond Briggs's second Christmas-themed book?

**2.** What is the name of Scrooge's clerk?

**3.** **Fill in the blank:** Complete the Dylan Thomas title, *A Child's Christmas in* _____ .

**4.** Who wrote *The Gift of the Magi*?

**5.** Which book was the inspiration for the classic Christmas movie *It's A Wonderful Life*?

**6.** Who is the baddie in *101 Dalmatians* by Dodie Smith?

**7.** Eloise is the star of which Christmas book, set in a New York hotel?

**8.** Most famous for *Meg and Mog*, Jan Pieńkowski wrote a Christmas pop-up book. What is the title?

**9.** **True or false?** Agatha Christie wrote *The Adventure of the Christmas Pudding*.

**10.** What is the name of Discworld's equivalent of Father Christmas?

**11.** **Fill in the blank:** Complete the John Updike title, *The Twelve _____ of Christmas*.

**12.** Where was Laura Ingalls Wilder's Christmas book set?

**13.** What is the title of Susan Cooper's classic fantasy book series which begins just before Christmas?

**14.** **Fill in the blank:** Complete the John Masefield title, *The Box of _____* .

**15.** **Fill in the blank:** Complete the Beatrix Potter classic from 1903, *The Tailor of _____* .

## Christmas Books

**1.** What is the title of David Sedaris's modern Christmas classic?

**2.** What was the name of Stella Gibbons' Christmas themed book set on a farm?

**3.** Who was the author of *The Life and Adventures of Santa Claus*?

**4.** Whose murder is central to Hercule Poirot's Christmas?

**5.** Who wrote *Rudolph the Red-Nosed Reindeer*?

**6.** Who saves Christmas in the book by Roddy Doyle?

**7.** How is the angel described in the title of the book by Christopher Moore?

**8.** Who wrote and illustrated the book *The Nightmare Before Christmas*?

**9.** What is the title of Sarah Morgan's 2020 Christmas-themed book?

**10.** What was the title of Truman Capote's famous Christmas book?

**11.** John Julius Norwich wrote of the 'ultimate Christmas' what?

**12.** Romance is rife in *One Day in December* by Josie Silver. Can you name the two protagonists?

**13.** What part of Britain is the setting of Ali Smith's *Winter*?

**14.** What does Kate Turner have twelve of in the book by Jenny Bayliss?

**15.** What is the name of the poem written by Maya Angelou about Christmas?

Answers on page 247

## General Knowledge

**1.** What colour are robin's eggs: blue or red?

**2.** **Fill in the blank:** Complete the famous pantomime title, _____ Whittington.

**3.** **True or false?** Whitney Houston never had a Christmas number one single.

**4.** In the Bible, who was king when Jesus was born?

**5.** What noise are turkeys said to make?

**6.** In _Home Alone_, where is Kevin's family going to spend Christmas?

**7.** **True or false?** Ben Miller wrote a book called _Diary of a Christmas Snowman_.

**8.** What is the name of a shiny decoration that wraps around a Christmas tree?

**9.** **Fill in the blank:** Complete the song title, 'In the _____ Midwinter'.

**10.** What is a common abbreviation for the word Christmas?

**11.** **True or false?** Midnight Mass is celebrated on New Year's Eve.

**12.** In *Elf*, who is Buddy's real father?

**13.** Where would you find Christmas Island?
 **a** Atlantic Ocean
 **b** Indian Ocean
 **c** North Sea
 **d** Pacific Ocean

**14.** **True or false?** A Christmas pudding is traditionally fried.

**15.** **True or false?** There is usually an elf in a nativity scene.

# Quiz 13

## General Knowledge

1. **True or false?** Queen Elizabeth performed in pantomimes during World War Two.

2. In the movie *A Christmas Story*, what does Ralphie want more than anything?

3. **Fill in the blank:** Complete the title, *A Christmas Carol in Prose: A _____ _____ of Christmas*.

4. What is traditionally shouted to give away the location of a pantomime villain?

5. Where does The Polar Express stop first in the story?

6. Who did the Weasley twins use magic to throw snowballs at in *Harry Potter and the Philosopher's Stone*?

7. In Iceland, there is a famous big, black Christmas what?

8. On what date is Christmas Eve in Serbia?

9. In Norse mythology, who flew through the sky delivering presents?

10. **True or false?** Shoe the Moo was a popular Elizabethan Christmas game.

**11.** What Christmas decoration represents the crown of thorns worn by Jesus?

**12.** According to Icelandic legend, what giant feline eats anyone who has not received new clothes for Christmas?

**13.** **True or false?** In France you can eat sweets in the shape of baby Jesus.

**14.** In what year was the first tree lighting ceremony at the Rockefeller Center in New York?

**15.** In what country do people hide their brooms on Christmas Eve to prevent wizards and witches from riding them?

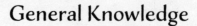

# Quiz 13

## General Knowledge

1. Who wrote the first Empire Address, a message from the royal family, in 1932?

2. Which British royal famously had a huge feast on Christmas Day in 1264?

3. What happened to Charles Dickens' last Christmas turkey?

4. Which country set a Guinness World Record for the largest surfing lesson with everyone dressed as Santa?

5. Who received the first official Christmas card sent in England?

6. In what year was Queen Elizabeth II's first speech televised?

7. In Catalonia, Spain, what does *El Caganer* do in the nativity scene?

8. What is it good luck to find in a Danish *risalamande*?

9. What is the Swedish Gävle Goat made from?

10. If you are mummering (or mumming), what do you visit?

**11.** Why would you assume Father Christmas's reindeer are female?

**12.** In Serbia, česnica is a type of what?

**13.** What do Annie Lennox, Justin Trudeau and Dido have in common?

**14.** On what day does Libya celebrate independence each year?

**15.** What is a *presepe*?

Answers on page 250

# Christmas Around the World

**1.** Where would you be if *Père Noël* delivered your presents?

**2.** Frumenty was a thick, porridge-like mixture that contained spices and dried fruit that was popular in Medieval times. What Christmas dessert did it inspire?

**3.** **True or false?** In Ireland families don't have Christmas trees.

**4.** In which European country do they celebrate *La Misa Del Gallo*, for the rooster that crowed when Jesus was born?

**5.** In the Netherlands, who is known as *Sinterklaas*?

**6.** In which country is it common to have a barbecue on Boxing Day?

**7.** Which country has presents delivered by the *Julemanden*; Denmark or Canada?

**8.** Which is the German equivalent of Happy Christmas?
   **a** Bitte Weihnachten
   **b** Frohe Schneemann
   **c** Frohe Weihnachten
   **d** Stille Weihnachten

**9.** Where is Santa known as *Santa-san*?
  **a** Japan
  **b** Ireland
  **c** New Zealand
  **d** Russia

**10.** In Greece it is common to see which of the below decorated at Christmas?
  **a** Apples
  **b** Boats
  **c** Chickens
  **d** Dumplings

**11.** **True or false?** In Switzerland, Santa is known as *Samichlaus*.

**12.** In Croatia, what does *Sretan Božić* mean?

**13.** Which Italian city is famous for its nativity scenes, known as *Presepe Napoletano*?

**14.** Where might you eat ackee, saltfish and curried goat at Christmas?

**15.** **True or false?** In Ukraine there are three Christmas Days.

Answers on page 251

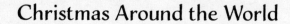

# Christmas Around the World

**1.** In France, on what date is the *Réveillon de Noël*?

**2.** Which saint is celebrated in Sweden on 13 December?

**3.** *Nollaig* is the word for Christmas in which language?

**4.** In Spain, 28 December is also known as the day of what?
a The Dead
b Extra Cake
c Innocent Saints
d Three Kings

**5.** **True or false?** It is a French tradition to eat Christmas dinner on Boxing Day.

**6.** Where would you be if you were wished a *Prettige Kerst*?

**7.** Where is Santa known as *Shengdan Laoren*?

**8.** In which country would you hear the greeting *Glædelig Jul*?

**9.** **True or false?** Eating fried chicken is a popular tradition in Japan at Christmas.

**10.** What colour clothes do the children celebrating Santa Lucia wear?

**11.** In Finland, what is different about Father Christmas (known as *Joulupukki*)?
  **a** She is a woman
  **b** He is a goat
  **c** He sleeps through Christmas
  **d** He eats the presents

**12.** In what country would you eat *kourabiedes* at Christmas?

**13.** **True or false?** The Swiss *grittibänz* is similar to a gingerbread man.

**14.** When do Christmas celebrations start in some parts of Croatia?
  **a** 1 November
  **b** 25 November
  **c** 1 December
  **d** 25 December

**15.** Where is Father Christmas known as *Pai Natal*?

## Christmas Around the World

1. What is *la crèche* in France at Christmas?

2. What is Father Christmas called in Germany?

3. In which European country would you encounter the Wren Boys Procession on Boxing Day?

4. What city in Germany is known as 'The Gingerbread Capital of the World'?

5. On what day does Sinterklaas visit in the Netherlands?

6. What fruit is given as a present on Christmas Eve in China?

7. What is the name of Netflix's Norwegian seasonal romcom series, which features main character Johanne and her search for a boyfriend?

8. What kind of cake is traditional to eat in Japan at Christmas?

9. Known as *lussekatt*, what type of buns are eaten in Sweden for Saint Lucia's day?

10. *Hyvää Joulua* is the equivalent of Happy Christmas in which country?

**11.** What type of food is *christopsomo*?

**12.** In Switzerland, what does Santa's helper *Schmutzli* carry?

**13.** In Ukraine, what is *koliadky*?

**14.** In what country do they say *Kala Christougenna*?

**15.** Cod is a traditional Christmas food in which European country?

# Quiz 15

## Christmas Drinks

1. **True or false?** Eggnog does not contain egg.

2. What is the name of the drink traditionally served to carol singers?
   a Brandy
   b Champagne
   c Singsong
   d Wassail

3. **Fill in the blank:** A winter drink often topped with marshmallows is called hot _____ .

4. Port is a popular drink at Christmas, but in which direction should you pass the bottle: left or right?

5. **True or false?** In some Scandinavian countries there is a drink called *sløbb*.

6. Complete the name of this drink, English Christmas...
   a Booze
   b Fizz
   c Punch
   d Slop

7. Is there such as drink as Coca-Cola Alexander?

8. **True or false?** Hot apple juice is added to whiskey to make a Hot Toddy.

9. **Fill in the blank:** Complete the drink, Hot Buttered _____ .

10. There is a special name for the bottle you put alcohol into when you go out. What is it?

11. Pimm's is a popular drink in the summer. What is the winter version known as?

12. Which country is Bailey's made in?

13. Which spirit is traditionally added when making a Christmas cake?

14. What colour is the drink Grinch Punch?

15. What animal is commonly featured in Coca-Cola's Christmas adverts?

Answers on page 254

# Quiz 15

## Christmas Drinks

1. What is often added to Eggnog?
   a Beer
   b Brandy
   c Lemonade
   d Wine

2. **True or false?** Wassail is traditionally served warm.

3. Hot Toddy is usually made with which juice?
   a Banana
   b Grape
   c Lemon
   d Milk

4. What is the name of the popular winter drink from Italy made with egg liqueur and brandy?

5. You drink an aperitif before a meal; what is the equivalent drink for after a meal?

6. **True or false?** English Christmas Punch is usually served warm.

7. What is the key non-alcoholic ingredient in a Brandy Alexander?

8. **True or false?** Buck's Fizz can be made with prosecco.

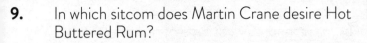

**9.** In which sitcom does Martin Crane desire Hot Buttered Rum?

**10.** What alcoholic drink is the most popular at the Christmas dinner table, according to a 2020 poll?

**11.** When was Baileys Original Irish Cream first introduced in the UK?
   **a** 1886
   **b** 1954
   **c** 1974
   **d** 2000

**12.** Tia Maria combines rum with what?

**13.** What fruit is central to Cointreau?

**14.** What is the UK's most popular champagne brand?

**15.** What drink was advertised at Christmas with a tree made of 140 empty barrels?

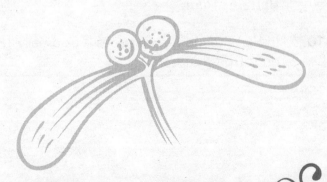

# Christmas Drinks

**1.** Eggnog is what type of milk drink?

**2.** What bowl is wassail traditionally served in?

**3.** Which spirit is used in a Hot Toddy?

**4.** What two drinks are often mulled?

**5.** In Sweden, what do you commonly place in the bottom of your glass before adding glögg?

**6.** In *A Christmas Carol*, what drink does Scrooge want to share with Bob Cratchit at the end of the book?

**7.** What can you add to a Brandy Alexander to make a Frozen Brandy Alexander?

**8.** What American cocktail is most similar to Buck's Fizz?

**9.** What book, published in 1937, popularised Hot Buttered Rum?

**10.** In *Rick and Morty*, what does Rick usually drink from?

**11.** What brand is the classic (and heavily advertised) advocaat used to make a Snowball?

**12.** Which of the following has NOT been released as a variant of Baileys Original Irish Cream?
   **a** Apple pie
   **b** Red velvet cupcake
   **c** Pumpkin spice
   **d** Rum and raisin

**13.** Tia Maria originated from which island?

**14.** In which city does Moët & Chandon have their head office?

**15.** Which beer once had a Christmas advert that featured Santa's reindeers drinking it?

# Quiz 16

## Festive Feasts

**1.** What pies are most popular at Christmas?

**2.** What non-edible plants are sometimes put on top of a Christmas pudding for decoration?

**3.** A southern African delicacy called mopane is which of the below?
a Chocolate
b Lamb
c Wildebeest
d Worm

**4.** **Fill in the blank:** A popular Christmas dessert is a Yule _____ .

**5.** Which green vegetable is believed to originate from Belgium?

**6.** What new (to him) fizzy drink does Elf enjoy in the movie?

**7.** Turrón is often served in Spain at Christmas. What is it?
a A drink
b Fruit
c Nougat
d Sherbet

**8.** **True or false?** Beetroot soup is a popular Christmas dish in Mexico.

**9.** Popular in Greece, baklava is made with honey, nuts and which type of pastry?

**10.** Turkey is the most popular meat on Christmas tables in the UK; what is the second most popular?

**11.** In Germany, which bird is it popular to eat at Christmas?

**12.** Does plum pudding contain plums?

**13.** In Sweden, are saffron buns or Princess Cakes more popular at Christmas?

**14.** Approximately how many mince pies are eaten in Britain each year?
 **a** 781
 **b** 781,000
 **c** 78,000,000
 **d** 781,000,000

**15.** Where in the world might you barbecue prawns and seafood at Christmas?

# Festive Feasts

**1.** In what country are the honey cookies known as *melomakarono* popular at Christmas time?

**2.** What is the Norwegian dish *smalahove*?

**3.** How many fish do you eat in the 'Feast of the _____ Fishes' in Italy?

**4.** In Iceland, *hangikjöt* is the traditional Christmas meal; what animal is it made from?

**5.** What sort of tarts are popular in Canada at Christmas?

**6.** What is the name of the famous German cake made with dried fruit and marzipan?

**7.** Where is hot fruit pudding a festive treat?

**8.** What is the name of the traditional Italian sponge cake that is served at Christmas?

**9.** *Julekake* is a traditional Christmas bread from which country?
   **a** Iceland
   **b** Norway
   **c** Portugal
   **d** Sweden

**10.** What is the name of a traditional Christmas bread in Bulgaria?

   **a** *Goosa*
   **b** *Kolivo*
   **c** *Pitka*
   **d** *Yumyum*

**11.** What is a *bûche de Noël* and in which country would you eat it?

**12.** How many courses might you be served at a traditional Christmas meal in Ukraine?

**13.** **True or false?** The traditional Lithuanian meal, *kūčios*, is served cold.

**14.** In what European country would you find *kołaczki* at Christmas?

**15.** **True or false?** In Costa Rica, tamales are not eaten at Christmas.

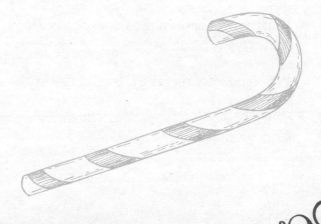

# Quiz 16

## Festive Feasts

**1.** In which European country is the dish *selyodka pod shuboy* commonly found at Christmas?

**2.** In Greenland, the raw hide of which animal is a festive delicacy?

**3.** Denmark's *risalamande* is similar to which English dessert?

**4.** In which country are *ping'anguo*, or peace apples, gifted on Christmas Eve?

**5.** What special cake would you eat in Mexico on *Día de Los Reyes*?

**6.** What seeds are found in the Irish Seed Cake that's popular at Christmas?

**7.** Where would you be at Christmas if you were eating *sochivo*?

**8.** What sort of cake is traditionally served in Jamaica at Christmas?

**9.** Which country serves a *julbord* at Christmas?

**10.** What type of fish is *bacalao*, a Mexican Christmas delicacy?

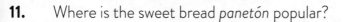

**11.** Where is the sweet bread *panetón* popular?

**12.** In which European country would you be if you ate fish soup and fried carp at Christmas?

**13.** *Lanttulaatikko*, a type of swede casserole, is popular in which country?

**14.** Where is Christmas Eve sometimes referred to as *Sowans Nicht*, after the meal made of soaked oat husks?

**15.** Which cousin of Eggnog, made with coconut milk and cinnamon, is popular in Puerto Rico?

# Quiz 17

## Christmas Decorations

**1.** What are the spherical objects often used to decorate Christmas trees called?

**2.** What is the name more commonly given to the big socks left out for Father Christmas to fill with presents?

**3.** **Fill in the blank:** Complete the title of the popular book and toy, _____ on the Shelf.

**4.** What is NOT commonly found on the top of a Christmas tree?
   **a** Angel
   **b** Bow
   **c** Owl
   **d** Star

**5.** What is the name of the item you hang on your front door at Christmas?

**6.** It is common to decorate the outside of a house with coloured what at Christmas?

**7.** Are Christmas trees evergreen or deciduous?

**8.** **True or false?** There is a law in England that states you must not decorate a Christmas tree before Christmas Eve.

**9.** What type of bag does Father Christmas carry his presents in?

**10.** **True or false?** Baubles are only ever red and green.

**11.** What long piece of cloth might you use to decorate presents after wrapping?

**12.** **True or false?** It used to be common to decorate Christmas trees with lit candles.

**13.** In India, what type of tree is commonly used as a Christmas tree?
  **a** Fir tree
  **b** Gum tree
  **c** Oak tree
  **d** Mango tree

**14.** Claridge's Hotel in London is famous for decorating what every Christmas?

**15.** **True or false?** Traditionally baubles were made from metal.

# Christmas Decorations

1. **Fill in the blank:** Complete the name of the traditional candle-based decoration, _____ chimes.

2. How many advent candles are lit before Christmas, traditionally?

3. **True or false?** In Ukraine it is considered lucky to find a cobweb in a Christmas tree.

4. In Norway, trees are decorated with *julekurver* baskets. What do they often contain?

5. Which European country is widely credited with the global popularity of the Christmas tree?

6. In Sweden, what does the person who symbolises Santa Lucia decorate their crown with?

7. **True or false?** Christmas crackers originally contained coins.

8. In Mexico, what might you hit with a stick to celebrate Christmas?

**9.** What is the most common shape for the paper window decorations that are common in Scandinavia at Christmas?

**10.** Which country donates the tree that is displayed every year in London's Trafalgar Square?

**11.** What two colours are traditional around Christmas in Argentina?

**12.** When first invented, what was tinsel made from?

**13.** What do you call the candles that are lit in the weeks running up to Christmas Day?

**14.** Since the 1960s, what sweet item has been created each year for display in the White House?

**15.** What colour is the candle traditionally placed in the window on Christmas Eve in Ireland?

Answers on page 261

# Quiz 17

## Christmas Decorations

1. In parts of Spain, the traditional nativity scene has an extra member. What are they called?

2. In Sweden, a giant creature made of straw decorates the town square. What is the creature and in which town can it be found?

3. Which city in Germany is particularly famous for its wreaths?

4. What is the name of the Swedish horse decorations that are popular at Christmas?

5. In Finland, ornate decorations called *himmeli* are made at Christmas. Traditionally, what are they made from?

6. In the Philippines, there is a festival of giant what every Christmas?

7. In New Zealand, what sort of tree is popular at Christmas?

8. According to Danish tradition, who decorates your house for Christmas?

9. In Barbados, baked ham is decorated with what fruit in a traditional Christmas meal?

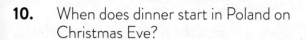

**10.** When does dinner start in Poland on Christmas Eve?

**11.** What do children in Holland leave out for Sinterklaas to put presents into?

**12.** What is the name of the small candle often used for Christmas decorations?

**13.** What is a *nacimiento*, popular in many Spanish-speaking countries?

**14.** What is placed under the tablecloth at the Christmas table in some European countries, including Lithuania?

**15.** Where in New York is there a famously big Christmas tree and a skating rink each Christmas?

Answers on page 262

# Christmas Trivia

**1.** Christmas is the celebration of whose birth?

**2.** Which of the following is an ancient term for Christmas?
**a** Feast-day
**b** Present Day
**c** Jesus's Birthday
**d** Yule

**3.** In what language does *Navidad* mean Christmas: German or Spanish?

**4.** **True or false?** The first Christmas celebration was in Egypt in 2000BCE.

**5.** In the nativity story, which angel visited Mary?

**6.** From which language is the word Noël taken?

**7.** In the UK, is it most common to open your presents on 6 December, 25 December or 31 December?

**8.** In the UK, what do people call the day after Christmas Day?

**9.** In the UK, what do people call the day before Christmas Day?

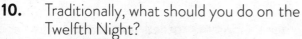

**10.** Traditionally, what should you do on the Twelfth Night?
- **a** Eat a Christmas dinner
- **b** Take down Christmas decorations
- **c** Open your presents
- **d** Bake a Christmas cake

**11.** **True or false?** Good Friday is the last Friday before Christmas.

**12.** The word nativity comes from the Latin *nativus*. What does that translate to?
- **a** King
- **b** Miracle
- **c** Star
- **d** Born

**13.** What was the name of Mary's husband?

**14.** On what day in 1066 was William crowned King of England?
- **a** Christmas Eve
- **b** Christmas Day
- **c** Boxing Day
- **d** New Years Day

**15.** **True or false?** Christmas was banned in England in the 17th century.

# Christmas Trivia

**1.** What is Christmas called in Italian?

**2.** What is the season leading up to Christmas called?

**3.** Which of the following is not related to Christmas?
a Advent
b The birth of Jesus
c The crucifixion of Jesus
d Three Wise Men

**4. True or false?** Christmas takes place around the summer solstice.

**5.** In 2015, a school in London set the Guinness World Record for longest Christmas cracker pulling chain. How many people took part?
a 987
b 1,000
c 1,077
d 1,093

**6.** What is the name of the piece of wood that is burned at Christmas in certain countries?

**7.** What are the two main components of a Christingle?

**8.** What play tells the story of the birth of Jesus?

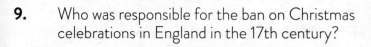

**9.** Who was responsible for the ban on Christmas celebrations in England in the 17th century?

**10.** **True or false?** Christmas Day is not a federal holiday (bank holiday) in the US.

**11.** Which of the following is not a real place in Pennsylvania, USA?
**a** Bethlehem
**b** Nativity
**c** Nazareth
**d** Galilee

**12.** What festive treat was believed to help women find themselves a husband in Tudor times?

**13.** **True or false?** All churches celebrate Christmas on the same day around the world.

**14.** At which famous monument was the winter solstice famously celebrated thousands of years ago?
**a** Grime's Graves
**b** Stonehenge
**c** The Tower of London
**d** Windsor Castle

**15.** What is the term used for a tip given to a tradesman (or servant in the past) at Christmas?

## Christmas Trivia

**1.** In religious terms, what does the Twelfth Night mark the beginning of?

**2.** Who do the angels speak to first in 'The First Noel'?

**3.** In which US city was the celebration of Christmas banned from 1659 to 1681?

**4.** Where would you be if you met *Ded Moroz*?

**5.** Traditionally, which way should you stir a Christmas pudding?

**6.** In what year was *A Christmas Carol* published?

**7.** Who sang the 1986 hit 'Driving Home for Christmas'?

**8.** What country do candy canes originate from?

**9.** What fruit was traditionally placed in a Christmas stocking?

**10.** On what day did my true love send me pipers piping (among other things)?

**11.** Where did we first hear about the reindeers Comet, Cupid, Donner and Blitzen?

**12.** Which holiday was the song 'Jingle Bells' originally written for?

**13.** What would you remove from your house on Saint Knut's Day, 13 January?

**14.** On what day is Christ's birth in the Gregorian calendar?

**15.** Which book, first published in 1955, features in the bestseller charts each year around Christmas?

# Quiz 19

## General Knowledge

1. In which US city does the movie *Godmothered* take place?
   a New York
   b Los Angeles
   c Boston
   d Chicago

2. Who visits the narrator in ''Twas the Night Before Christmas'?

3. What animal was the star of *The Flight Before Christmas* in 2021?

4. What is the name of the first church service on Christmas Day?
   a Cheerful Carols
   b Evensong
   c Midnight Mass
   d Midnight Party

5. **True or false?** The official name for Brussels sprouts is Fairy Cabbages.

6. Would you place a star at the top or bottom of a Christmas tree?

7. **Fill in the blank:** Complete the pantomime title, *Puss in _____ .*

**8.** According to the book, how many days does Phileas Fogg have to travel around the world?

**9.** What is the name of the snowman in *Frozen*?

**10.** **Fill in the blank:** Complete the title of the TV show that has become a Christmas classic in the UK, *Call the _____* .

**11.** In the popular carol, what did the shepherds watch by night?

**12.** Where would you expect to find your Elf, according to the 2005 book?

**13.** Where would you be if someone wished you *Joyeux Noël*?

**14.** **True or false?** Father Christmas has always been depicted in a red suit.

**15.** Where did the cast of *Harry Potter and the Philosopher's Stone* return to at Christmas in 2021?

# Quiz 19

## General Knowledge

1. **Fill in the blank:** Complete the 2021 Christmas romcom title, _____ *All The Way*.

2. What is the name of Scrooge's deceased business partner in *A Christmas Carol*?

3. Which children's classic was filmed and broadcast for the first time at Christmas in 2021?
   a *The Gruffalo*
   b *The Highway Rat*
   c *The Polar Express*
   d *Superworm*

4. Who was crowned King of England on Christmas Day in 1066?

5. What links Dido, Shane McGowan and Chris Kamara?

6. **True or false?** In medieval times, people would eat roast peacock at Christmas.

7. What is a Christmas nutcracker most commonly dressed as?

8. What position does Dick Whittington hold by the end of the pantomime?

**9.** Which island-set police show got a Christmas special for the first time in 2021?

**10. Fill in the blank:** Complete the name of the classic American Christmas cartoon, first broadcast in 1965, *A _____ _____ Christmas*.

**11. Fill in the blank:** Complete the carol title, 'Good Christian Men _____'.

**12.** From which country did *Elf on the Shelf* originate?

**13.** In what year was *The Snowman and the Snowdog* first broadcast?

**14. True or false?** In Argentina, gifts can be brought by *Papá Noel* (Father Christmas) or *El Niño Diós* (baby Jesus).

**15.** On what day was the *Doctor Who* special shown in 2021?

# Quiz 19

## General Knowledge

1. In *Last Christmas*, what Christmas character does Katarina dress as when she's at work?

2. What is the name of Scrooge's sister in *A Christmas Carol*?

3. On what day was the *Great British Bake Off Christmas Special* aired in 2021?

4. What did George Washington famously cross on Christmas Day in 1776?

5. What links Lars Ulrich, Conor Mason and Kit Harrington?

6. What is the name of the book written in 1816 by E. T. A. Hoffmann, later turned in a ballet?

7. According to US scientists, how many homes would Father Christmas need to visit a second in order to deliver every present on Christmas Eve?

8. What is the name of the pantomime dame in *Aladdin*?

9. Who played Worzel Gummidge in the 2021 BBC adaptation?

**10.** What animated Christmas classic lost out to *Toy Story 4* at the Academy Awards® in 2020?

**11.** What is the chemical formula for snow?

**12.** Who are the authors of *The Elf on the Shelf*?

**13.** Where would you be if someone wishes you *Mele Kalikimaka*?

**14.** What does *Julemanden* mean, literally, in Danish?

**15.** *The Larkins* (2021) is an adaptation of which novel?

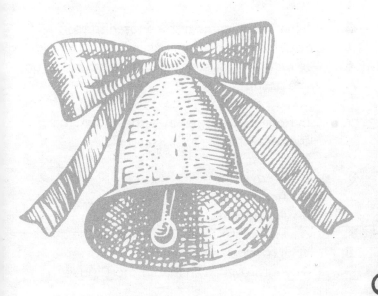

# Quiz 20

## Christmas Animations

**1.** What Christmas classic about a magical train journey features Tom Hanks?

**2.** In *Arthur Christmas*, what is the name of the current Santa?

**3.** What is the name of the 2018 animated movie based on the Dr. Seuss book, *How the Grinch Stole Christmas*?

**4.** **Fill in the blank:** Complete the title of the 2012 movie that featured Santa Claus teaming up with Jack Frost, the Easter Bunny and the Tooth Fairy, *Rise of the* _____ .

**5.** What is the name of the *Frozen* sequel?

**6.** In *Klaus*, who is sent to Smeerensburg to run the post office?

**7.** In *Robin Robin*, what bird does Robin make friends with?
   **a** A seagull
   **b** A crow
   **c** An eagle
   **d** A magpie

**8.** Which *Frozen* character had a 'Frozen Adventure' in an animated short movie?

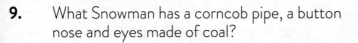

**9.** What Snowman has a corncob pipe, a button nose and eyes made of coal?

**10.** What two books are combined to make the story of the animated film *Father Christmas*, that was first broadcast on TV in the UK in 1991?

**11.** What holiday, other than Christmas, is featured in *The Nightmare Before Christmas*?

**12.** Who is 'the most famous reindeer of them all', with his own animated movie?

**13.** In *Mickey's Christmas Carol*, who plays Scrooge?

**14.** **True or false?** There is an Elf on the Shelf movie, called *The Elf on the Shelf Goes Wild For Christmas*.

**15.** What is the name of the Troll King in *Frozen*?

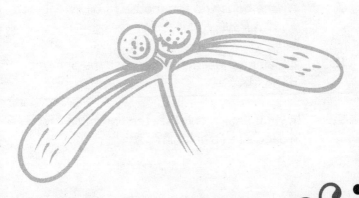

Answers on page 269

# Christmas Animations

**1.** What is the name of the spaceship that is used to deliver presents in *Arthur Christmas*?

**2.** What movie holds the Guinness World Record for longest digital performance capture?

**3.** Who voiced the Grinch in the animated movie *The Grinch*?

**4.** Who joins the Guardians at the end of *Rise of the Guardians*?

**5.** Who of the following is not in *Frozen 2*?
  **a** Anna
  **b** Elsa
  **c** Olaf
  **d** Prince Hans

**6.** In *Klaus*, how many letters does the hero have to post in a year to be a success?

**7.** Whose house do the mouse family steal food from in *Robin Robin*?

**8.** Which channel first broadcast *The Snowman* in the UK?

**9.** In what year was *Frosty the Snowman* first broadcast in the USA?

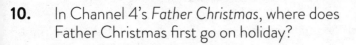

**10.** In Channel 4's *Father Christmas*, where does Father Christmas first go on holiday?

**11.** Where does Jack Skellington live in *The Nightmare Before Christmas*?

**12.** **True or false?** The 1964 animation *Rudolph the Red-Nosed Reindeer* was the first time the character was mentioned.

**13.** In the 1983 animation *Mickey's Christmas Carol*, who plays Bob Cratchit?

**14.** What ran over Grandma in the 2000 animation (and the famous song)?

**15.** What are the names of the three main characters in *Tokyo Godfathers*, set on Christmas Eve?

# Quiz 20

## Christmas Animations

1. Who voiced the narrator in 2018's *The Grinch*?

2. What is the name of the Santa Claus character in *Rise of the Guardians*?

3. Which month in 2019 was the first *Frozen 2* trailer released?

4. What are the names of the two feuding families in *Klaus*?

5. In *Robin Robin*, who voices the part of the cat?

6. Raymond Briggs wrote Christmas classic *The Snowman*, but can you name his book about a nuclear attack on Britain, later turned into an animated movie?

7. What is the name of the magician in the 1969 Christmas special *Frosty the Snowman*?

8. What is the title of the 2016 Disney Christmas animation featuring Mickey Mouse?

9. Where is the baby found at the start of *Tokyo Godfathers*?

**10.** What is Jack Skellington's official title in *The Nightmare Before Christmas*?

**11.** In the 1964 movie *Rudolph the Red-Nosed Reindeer*, who is Rudolph's father?

**12.** In *Mickey's Christmas Carol*, who plays the ghost of Jacob Marley?

**13.** Which popular character's Christmas animation first premiered in the USA in 1965?

**14.** What was the name of the sequel to *Mickey's Once Upon A Christmas*?

**15.** *Frozen* won two Academy Awards® in 2014; what were they?

# Quiz 21

## Christmas Songs

1. **Fill in the blank:** Complete the classic song title, 'I Wish It Could Be Christmas _____'.

2. **True or false?** Mariah Carey's 'All I Want For Christmas Is You' has never been a Christmas number one in the UK or USA.

3. What kind of Aid has been a Christmas number one in the UK more than once?

4. Which band had a Christmas hit with the song 'Christmas Time (Don't Let the Bells End)'?

5. What Christmas song was released by Wham! in 1984?

6. **Fill in the blank:** Complete the Christmas song title, 'Fairytale of _____ _____'.

7. **True or false?** Bob the Builder recorded one of the 20 bestselling Christmas records of all time.

8. What was the title of LadBaby's 2020 Christmas song?

9. A song featured in *Frozen* asks if you want to build a what?

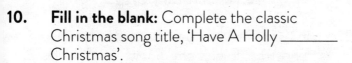

**10.** **Fill in the blank:** Complete the classic Christmas song title, 'Have A Holly _____ Christmas'.

**11.** In 2019 John Legend had a top 10 Christmas hit with the song 'Happy Xmas (War is Over)', but who originally released the song in 1971?

**12.** 'Feliz Navidad' was a hit for José Feliciano but in what language does it mean Merry Christmas?

**13.** What was the name of Ariana Grande's 2014 Christmas song?

**14.** In 2017 the same artist was at Christmas number one and featured on the number two single. Who was it?
  **a** LadBaby
  **b** George Michael
  **c** Eminem
  **d** Ed Sheeran

**15.** Who sang 'Mistletoe and Wine'?

# Christmas Songs

1. In 1973, Slade topped the charts with 'Merry Christmas Everybody' but what other classic song was also in the top five that year?

2. What is the name of the Mariah Carey album that featured 'All I Want For Christmas Is You'?

3. Who wrote the song 'Do They Know It's Christmas?'?

4. Who pipped The Darkness to the Christmas number one slot in the UK in 2003?

5. **True or false?** 'Last Christmas' by Wham! was the biggest-selling single that did not hit the Christmas number one slot in the UK.

6. 'Fairytale of New York' featured Kirsty MacColl but can you name her famous father?

7. What is number two on the list of the UK's bestselling Christmas records of all time?

8. **True or false?** In 2021, Wham!'s 'Last Christmas' was number two at Christmas in the UK charts.

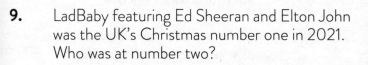

**9.** LadBaby featuring Ed Sheeran and Elton John was the UK's Christmas number one in 2021. Who was at number two?

**10.** According to the classic Gene Autry Christmas song, here comes who?

**11.** What is the name of Justin Bieber's bestselling Christmas hit from 2011?

**12.** **True or false?** Wham!'s 'Last Christmas' is a big holiday hit in the USA.

**13.** What song held the number two slot in the UK at Christmas in 2019?

**14.** Who sang 'Man's Not Hot', a Christmas top ten in the UK charts in 2017?

**15.** 'Always On My Mind' was a Christmas number one for the Pet Shop Boys but who was the song a hit for in 1972?

# Quiz 21

## Christmas Songs

1. What year did the Pet Shop Boys top the UK Christmas chart with 'Always On My Mind'?

2. What year did Mariah Carey's 'All I Want For Christmas Is You' first top the US charts at Christmas?

3. Which member of *The Young Ones* appeared at the recording for Band Aid's 'Do They Know It's Christmas?'?

4. What is the name of the lead singer in The Darkness?

5. What song kept Wham! from the number one slot in the UK at Christmas in 1984?

6. What is odd about the NYPD choir as mentioned in the song 'Fairytale of New York'?

7. Wings' Christmas hit 'Mull of Kintyre' was a double A-side in 1977; what was the other song?

8. In 2021, how many of the UK's top 10 singles at Christmas featured the word 'Christmas' in the title?

**9.** What is LadBaby's real name?

**10.** In what movie does Judy Garland sing 'Have Yourself A Very Merry Christmas'?

**11.** In what year was 'Rockin' Around the Christmas Tree' a hit for Brenda Lee in the US?

**12.** In 2008 'Hallelujah' held both number one and two spots in the Christmas charts. Who were the artists?

**13.** How many spots did Stormzy hold in the top 10 UK singles chart at Christmas in 2019?

**14.** What was the second of the Spice Girls' trio of Christmas number ones?

**15.** What song links Leonard Cohen and Pentatonix?

# Quiz 22

## Christmas Traditions

1. In South Africa at Christmas you might eat Braai. What is it?
   a Barbecue
   b Hog roast
   c Turkey
   d Cured meat

2. How many doors are there typically to open on an advent calendar?

3. **True or false?** In Finland it is the law to have a sauna on Christmas Day.

4. According to legend in the Czech Republic, who delivers presents to children?

5. In France, would you eat or drink a *Bûche de Noël*?

6. What colourful article of clothing might you wear to work or school in the run up to Christmas?

7. In Russia, how many days do some people fast before Christmas; 14 or 40 days?

8. In the USA, where are presents usually left on Christmas Eve?

134

**9.** **True or false?** In Greenland there is a seasonal speciality called Yukyuk.

**10.** What icy activity on rinks is popular at Christmas?

**11.** What has become a tradition on Christmas Day for some people in coastal towns in the UK?
   **a** Drive to the supermarket
   **b** Swim in the sea
   **c** Knit a giant scarf
   **d** Run a marathon

**12.** **True or false?** *Grosso Rosso* is another name for Father Christmas in Italy.

**13.** There is a festive-named town in Florida, USA. What is it called?
   **a** Christmas
   **b** Elf Town
   **c** Santa's Grotto
   **d** Snowville

**14.** Where do the Yule Lads of Iceland leave a rotten potato for children if they have not been good?

**15.** What type of fish will often be found on the Christmas dinner table in Portugal; cod or tuna?

# Christmas Traditions

1.  In Venezuela, what form of transport has become common to get to Church at Christmas?
    a   Bicycle
    b   Pogo stick
    c   Roller skates
    d   Sleigh

2.  **True or false?** In Indonesia, a special type of Christmas tree is made from chicken feathers.

3.  *Bolo Rei* is a popular food in Portugal at Christmas; what type of food is it?

4.  In Wales, what do you sing at a *Plygain* service?

5.  In the Czech Republic, women tell their fortunes at Christmas by throwing which of the following behind them; a cake, some salt or a shoe?

6.  In what country would you find spider webs in your tree as a traditional decoration?
    a   Ireland
    b   South Africa
    c   Romania
    d   Ukraine

**7.** In what country does Sooty Piet accompany Sinterklaas?

**8.** In Spain, when do you eat 12 grapes for your good luck and fortune?

**9.** **True or false?** In Russia, the 12 days of Christmas begin in January.

**10.** In what language does *Boas Festas* mean Merry Christmas?

**11.** What sort of house is often built in the USA at Christmas?

**12.** In what country would you eat a traditional dish of auk fermented in a seal skin?

**13.** According to tradition in the Netherlands, where does Santa Claus put naughty children?

**14.** In 2015 a messy board game became a Christmas sensation; what was it called?

**15.** In what year was *Die Hard* released?

## Christmas Traditions

**1.** In Portugal, when would you eat *consoada*?

**2.** In Wales, what is the *Mari Lwyd*?

**3.** According to Finnish folklore, who uses the sauna after sunset on Christmas Eve?

**4.** In the Czech Republic which fruit do you traditionally cut after Christmas dinner to tell your future?

**5.** In Spain, what colour underwear is supposed to bring you love if worn at New Year?

**6.** In Russia, what is the name of the period between Orthodox Christmas and Epiphany?

**7.** In parts of the USA, what decoration would you hope to find on the Christmas tree as the first to spot it will have good luck?

**8.** Traditionally, how many dishes are served at dinner on Christmas Eve in Poland?

**9.** In Iceland, how many Yule Lads are there?

**10.** At a traditional Portuguese Christmas meal you may lay more places than there are people. Who are the extra places for?

**11.** Who sent the first official Christmas card in the UK?

**12.** What is *pepernoot*, popular in the Netherlands at Christmas parties?

**13.** For which US department store was Rudolph the Red-Nosed Reindeer originally created?

**14.** In Oaxaca, Mexico, what vegetable is carved on 23 December?

**15.** What type of food is *cougnou*?

# Quiz 23

## Nativity

1. Where did Mary and Joseph live before the birth of Jesus?

2. **True or false?** Joseph was a shepherd.

3. In what town was Jesus born?

4. What did the Wise Men follow in order to find the baby Jesus?
   a  A map
   b  The leader
   c  A star
   d  The Yellow Brick Road

5. Why did Mary and Joseph not stay at an inn?

6. Who visited the baby Jesus first, shepherds or Wise Men?

7. What did the Three Wise Men give to the baby Jesus?

8. How did Mary and Joseph travel to Bethlehem?

9. What did Mary put Jesus into after he was born?

10. **True or false?** The song 'Little Donkey' features in the Bible.

**11.** Which male actor starred as a teacher in the 2009 film *Nativity!*?

**12.** What nativity-themed, animated movie featuring a song by Mariah Carey was released in 2017?

**13.** **True or false?** There is a devil figure in a traditional nativity scene in the UK.

**14.** **Fill in the blank:** Complete the title of the famous song, 'The Little _____ Boy'.

**15.** Name one animal you often see in a nativity scene.

# Quiz 23

## Nativity

1. Which of the below is Mary known as?
   a Blessed Virgin Mary
   b Most Blessed Mary
   c Revered Virgin Mother
   d Admired Mary Mother

2. The Three Wise Men are also referred to by what name?

3. What does the song 'Little Donkey' describe?

4. What is a manger?

5. What did the king order for all the boys in Bethlehem?

6. Why was Bethlehem so busy on the night of Jesus's birth?

7. In *Love Actually*, what animal does Harry and Karen's daughter play in the nativity?

8. What was the first sequel to *Nativity!* called?

9. **Fill in the blank:** Complete the title of the epic movie from 1965, *The Greatest _____ Ever Told*.

**10.** **True or false?** Oprah Winfrey one voiced a camel in a Christmas movie.

**11.** In what 1959 movie starring Charlton Heston is the nativity (briefly) covered?

**12.** Who played the part of the mayor in *Nativity!*?

**13.** In what film is a character called Brian mistaken for the messiah?

**14.** Which bakery chain replaced the baby Jesus with a sausage roll in their advent calendar in 2017?

**15.** Who sang 'The Little Drummer Boy' in duet with Bing Crosby?

## Nativity

1. Which biblical gospels tell the story of the nativity?

2. King Herod was also known as what?

3. Who was responsible for the conception of Jesus?

4. Approximately how long after the birth of Jesus was the first nativity play recorded?

5. Who is thought to have chosen 25 December as the birth date of Jesus?

6. Which animals are mentioned in the Bible as being present at the birth of Jesus?

7. What was the second sequel to the movie *Nativity!* called?

8. What was the third sequel to the movie *Nativity!* called?

9. What country is Bethlehem in?

10. What part did Christopher Plummer play in *The Star*?

11. In *The Greatest Story Ever Told*, what part did Sidney Poitier play?

**12.** According to the Bible, how many Wise Men visited Jesus?

**13.** What is the name of the church in Bethlehem that is acknowledged as the birthplace of Jesus?

**14.** What TV presenter and newsreader played himself in *Nativity!*?

**15.** Who played Jesus in *The Greatest Story Ever Told*?

# Quiz 24

## Christmas Sport

**1.** **True or false?** There are always Premier League football matches on TV on Christmas Day.

**2.** Every year in Orkney, two teams get together to play a mass game of street football called the Ba', but which two days do they play?
**a** Christmas Eve and New Year's Eve
**b** Christmas Day and New Year's Day
**c** Christmas Eve and New Year's Day
**d** Christmas Day and New Year's Eve

**3.** Which of the following is a formation in which a football team might play?
**a** Boxing Day
**b** Christmas 1-2-3
**c** Christmas Day
**d** Christmas Tree

**4.** What country holds a famous cricket match called the Boxing Day Test?

**5.** What Welsh footballer, who played for Arsenal and Juventus, was born on Boxing Day in 1990?

**6.** In what year was a football match played between German and British troops on Christmas Day, although they were at war?

**7.** **True or false?** NFL (American football) is never played on Christmas Day.

**8.** Which Chris, a former professional football player and now a pundit, was born on Christmas Day in 1957?

**9.** **Fill in the blank:** Complete the name of the Brazilian forward who first played for Manchester City in 2017, Gabriel _____ .

**10.** In what year was the first Football League match played on Christmas Day?
   **a** 1860
   **b** 1889
   **c** 1900
   **d** 1964

**11.** **True or false?** The NBA's tradition of Christmas Day basketball matches dates back to 1847.

**12.** Switzerland's 'ClauWau' is described as the world championships of what?
   **a** Elves
   **b** Postmen
   **c** Reindeer
   **d** Santas

**13.** **True or false?** In 1940 Tommy Lawton played a match for Everton on the morning of Christmas Day, then another for Tranmere in the afternoon.

**14.** **True or false?** Football matches were often played on Christmas Day in the Victorian era.

# Christmas Sport

**1.** In what year was the last professional football match played in Scotland on Christmas Day?
   **a** Football has never been played on Christmas Day in Scotland
   **b** 1914
   **c** 1963
   **d** 1973

**2.** In what year was a game in the South American Championship football tournament played on Christmas Day?

**3.** What is the name of the horse that won the 2,000 Guineas and the Irish Derby and was named British Horse of the Year in 1964?
   **a** Mr Christmas
   **b** Red Rum
   **c** Santa Claus
   **d** Shergar

**4.** What English cricketer was born on Christmas Day in 1984?

**5.** What famous royal event takes place at Sandringham on Boxing Day?

**6.** Who won the first Boxing Day Test match at the Melbourne Cricket Ground?

**7.** Sprinter Yohan Blake was born on Boxing Day in 1989. What country does he represent?

**8.** What footballer's playing career was ended on Boxing Day in 1962 through injury, but went on to win two European Cups as a manager?

**9.** Chelsea FC fielded a team on Boxing Day in 1999 that was the first of its kind. What was different about it?

**10.** On what 'land' did the famous England v Germany Christmas Day match during World War I take place?

**11.** Which Chicago Bulls player wore number 23 when they played the Knicks on Christmas Day in 1986?

**12.** In what year did the West Indies beat Australia in a Christmas Day Test Match in Adelaide?

**13.** What famous Scottish footballer, and captain, was born on Christmas Day in 1964?

**14.** What Olympic ski event, where style and tricks are paramount, was first introduced in the 2022 Winter Olympic Games?

**15.** **True or false?** Arsenal were prevented from playing matches on Christmas Day until 1950 because Highbury was built on religious ground.

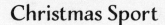

# Quiz 24

## Christmas Sport

**1.** What year was the last top level football match played on Christmas Day in England?

**2.** In what part of the UK is the Steel & Sons Cup final played on Christmas Day (unless it's a Sunday)?

**3.** What is the name of the steeplechase held at Kempton Park traditionally run on Boxing Day?

**4.** In what year did England last win the Boxing Day Test match at Melbourne Cricket Ground?

**5.** In what Scandinavian country is *Annandagsbandy*, a bandy game, traditionally played on Boxing Day?

**6.** In 1541, all sports were banned on Christmas Day in England, apart from one. What was it?

**7.** How many people attended the Boxing Day women's football match at Goodison Park in 1920?

**8.** Which famous cricketer, the first to play 100 Test matches for his country, was born on Christmas Eve in 1932?

**9.** Which two countries contested the Davis Cup tennis final in 1986, starting on Boxing Day?

**10.** Which is the highest football ground in terms of elevation in England and Wales?

**11.** What was the name of the rugby union competition held in November and December 2020?

**12.** In what year did the NHL stop Christmas Day ice hockey matches?

**13.** What was remarkable about the Christmas Day NFL game between the Miami Dolphins and the Kansas City Chiefs in 1971?

**14.** In what sport did Tommy Burns and Jack Johnson compete on Boxing Day 1908?

**15.** What was the nickname given to the famous 1977 Christmas Eve NFL playoff game between the Raiders and the Colts?

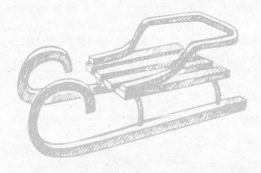

# Quiz 25

## General Knowledge

1. What is the more common name for a sausage wrapped in bacon?

2. What is the name of Bob Cratchit's son in *A Christmas Carol*?

3. What red-breasted bird has a common association with Christmas in the UK?

4. **True or false?** *Jack and the Giant Boots* is a famous pantomime.

5. What colour are the berries on mistletoe?

6. How many reindeer are named in "Twas the Night Before Christmas'?

7. Where does Postman Pat deliver post for Christmas?

8. **True or false?** *The Elf on the Shelf* is an old Christmas tradition, dating back to Victorian times.

9. What popular Christmas sweets are shaped like a shepherd's crook?

**10.** Kurt Russell played Santa Claus in which movie and its sequel?

   **a** *Santa Claus*
   **b** *A Boy Called Christmas*
   **c** *Arthur Christmas*
   **d** *The Christmas Chronicles*

**11.** Which of the Wise Men's gifts begins with F?

**12.** **True or false?** In Estonia it is common for a family to take a sauna together at Christmas.

**13.** What colour are the berries on holly?

**14.** What is Frosty the Snowman's nose made from?

**15.** In a pantomime what do audiences traditionally do when the villain comes on stage?

Answers on page 284

## General Knowledge

1. What meat is sometimes added to sprouts to give more flavour?

2. **True or false?** Tinsel was invented in England.

3. Which pantomime commonly includes a character called Buttons?

4. What is the name of the chocolate frog who appears in a selection box in the UK at Christmas?

5. In what town does *How the Grinch Stole Christmas* take place?

6. What is the world's bestselling Christmas single of all time?

7. What day does Scrooge allow Bob Cratchit to have off in *A Christmas Carol*?

8. In parts of central Europe, what is the name of the horned figure who punishes naughty children at Christmas?

9. What sauce (or butter) is the traditional accompaniment to Christmas pudding?

10. Which two Christmas movies have featured Goldie Hawn as Mrs Claus?

**11.** Where do Harry Potter and Hermione celebrate Christmas in *Harry Potter and the Deathly Hallows*?

**12.** What is the date of Saint Stephen's day?

**13.** One of Santa's reindeer has a 'love-ly' name. What is it?

**14.** What almond-flavoured food is commonly used to cover a Christmas cake?

**15.** What did confectioner and baker Tom Smith invent?
  **a** Christmas cards
  **b** Christmas pudding
  **c** Christmas crackers
  **d** Christmas cake

# Quiz 25

## General Knowledge

**1.** In what year was tinsel invented?

**2.** How is a Christmas pudding traditionally cooked?

**3.** Robins, often associated with Christmas cards in the UK, were originally representative of what?

**4.** In Catalonia what is *Caga Tío*, a tradition where this item is 'fed' with leftovers then beaten with a stick so it poops treats?

**5.** Two of Santa's reindeer are named after the German words for thunder and lightning. What are they?

**6.** How many ghosts visit Scrooge in *A Christmas Carol*?

**7.** What name is given to a female turkey?

**8.** Who visits children in the run up to Christmas in Iceland?

**9.** What day is American musician Jimmy Buffett's birthday?

**10.** What word describes the flower bud of an evergreen tree, used to add flavour to food?

**11.** Which song came first, 'Rudolph the Red-Nosed Reindeer' or 'Frosty the Snowman'?

**12.** What is the name of a celebration of African-American heritage and culture that begins on 26 December?

**13.** The movie *A Christmas Story* was based on which book?

**14.** In parts of Scandinavia, presents are delivered by a character called the *Jultomten*. What animals pull his sleigh?

**15.** If you were born on Christmas Day, what is your star sign?

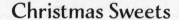

# Quiz 26

## Christmas Sweets

1. **Fill in the blank:** Complete the name of a Christmas favourite selection box, Milk _____ .

2. What chocolate selection box includes Milky Way, Galaxy, Bounty and Twix?

3. What do you find inside Quality Street's Purple One?

4. **True or false?** Cadbury Roses selection box includes a rose-flavoured chocolate.

5. Which selection box includes a mini Twirl, Dairy Milk and Wispa?
   a Cadbury Roses
   b Cadbury Heroes
   c Cadbury Superstars
   d Cadbury Zeroes

6. In Quality Street, what shape is the Green One?

7. **True or false?** In Cadbury Roses there is a chocolate called Golden Barrel.

8. Which of the following do you NOT find in Celebrations: Mars, Snickers or Milky Bar?

**9.** **Fill in the blank:** Complete the name of this Quality Street chocolate, Coconut _____.

**10.** Is a Quality Street Toffee Penny covered in chocolate?

**11.** Which of the following chocolates would you find in Cadbury Roses?
   **a** Strawberry Dream
   **b** Strawberry Nightmare
   **c** Strawberry Swirl
   **d** Strawberry Yumyum

**12.** Whose Chocolate Orange is a Christmas classic?

**13.** **Fill in the blank:** Complete the name of the Cadbury Heroes chocolate, Creme _____ _____.

**14.** **True or false?** You can only buy Celebrations at Christmas.

**15.** **True or false?** In Cadbury Roses there is a chocolate called Chocolate Banana Fudge Cake.

# Quiz 26

## Christmas Sweets

1. Which Christmas favourite featured the line 'you're really spoiling us' in the advertisements?

2. Which chocolate selection box featured the tagline 'all because the lady loves...'?

3. In 2020 what limited edition flavour went missing from Quality Street tins?
   a  Red Velvet Brownie
   b  Mint Choc Chip Brownie
   c  Chocolate Caramel Brownie
   d  Coconut Brownie

4. Which company invented Quality Street chocolates?

5. According to a YouGov poll in 2017, what is the most popular chocolate in Quality Street?

6. In Celebrations what is the name of the Malteser chocolate?

7. Quality Street's Noisette Triangle changed its name to what?

8. What do you find inside Cadbury Roses Golden Barrel?

9. What shape is Quality Street's Strawberry Delight?

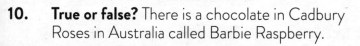

**10.** **True or false?** There is a chocolate in Cadbury Roses in Australia called Barbie Raspberry.

**11.** How many different chocolates are in Cadbury Heroes?

**12.** **Fill in the blank:** Complete the classic Cadbury Roses advertisement, 'Cadbury Roses grow on _____'.

**13.** In what year were Cadbury Roses launched?

**14.** **True or false?** There was a Quality Street chocolate called Peanut Cracker.

**15.** What colour are a box or tin of Cadbury Roses?

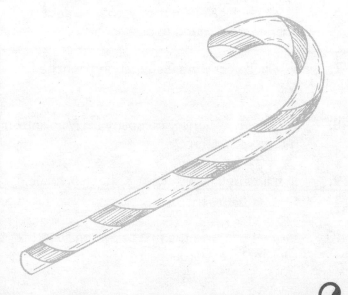

# Quiz 26

## Christmas Sweets

**1.** Cadbury Roses teamed up with which famous textile designer for a limited edition Christmas tin?

**2.** Quality Street chocolates were named after a play by which famous author?

**3.** What was the previous name for the Purple One in Quality Street?

**4.** What type of 'Darkness' would you find in Cadbury Roses?

**5.** What was Quality Street's famous tagline during the 1970s?

**6.** In which decade did the Quality Street tin change from round to octagonal?

**7.** In which year were Celebrations launched by Mars?

**8.** What confectionery company did Mackintosh merge with in 1969?

**9.** In Cadbury Heroes, what is the mini Double Decker named?

**10.** In what year was the first television advert for Quality Street broadcast?

**11.** What launched first, Dairy Milk or Bournville?

**12.** In which year did Cadbury Roses launch?

**13.** In what city is Quality Street produced?

**14.** What do Cadbury Dream, Fuse and Time Out have in common?

**15.** In which year were Quality Street launched?

## Christmas Characters

1. Who created the book *The Jolly Christmas Postman or Other People's Letters*?

2. Who works in Santa's workshop building toys?

3. **True or false?** In *The Snowman*, the characters visit places by train.

4. What is the full name of the main character in *Arthur Christmas*?

5. What is the name of the beloved cat who features in a Christmas story by Judith Kerr?
   - **a** Meg
   - **b** Maggie
   - **c** Madge
   - **d** Mog

6. In *The Polar Express*, who encourages the boy to get on the train?

7. What colour is the Grinch?

8. **True or false?** Pitch Black is a character in *Rise of the Guardians*.

9. In what book would you find the Snowdog?

**10.** **True or false?** Candy Woo Woo is a character in *How The Grinch Stole Christmas*.

**11.** In *Elf*, what is the name of the woman Buddy asks on a date?
   **a** Jodie
   **b** Elfie
   **c** Jovie
   **d** Jessica

**12.** What colour is the witch in *The Lion, The Witch and The Wardrobe*?

**13.** What is the name of the pig in *The Christmas Pig*?

**14.** What animal appears at Tilly's window in the Raymond Briggs classic?

**15.** What is the name of the main character in *The Girl Who Saved Christmas*?

## Christmas Characters

**1.** What is Jack's surname in *The Nightmare Before Christmas*?

**2.** **True or false?** The 1947 movie *Miracle on 34th Street* is in full colour.

**3.** What is the name of the popular teaching assistant in *Nativity!*?

**4.** Which actor plays Hans Gruber, the baddie in *Die Hard*?

**5.** **Fill in the blank:** Complete the movie title, *Christmas With The* _____ .

**6.** What is the name of the main Mogwai character in *Gremlins*?

**7.** Who plays the part of Karen in *Love Actually* and Petra Andrich in *Last Christmas*?

**8.** In what Christmas special would you find Yukon Cornelius?

**9.** What is the name of George Bailey's uncle in *It's A Wonderful Life*?

**10.** How many films are in the *Die Hard* series?

**11.** What is the name of Scrooge's nephew in *A Christmas Carol*?

**12. Fill in the blank:** Complete the title of this 1985 Disney Christmas movie, *One _____ Christmas*.

**13.** What is the name of Arthur Claus's older brother in *Arthur Christmas*?

**14.** What type of festive tree did Julia Donaldson write a book about?

**15.** What is the name of Charlie Brown's sister?

## Christmas Characters

1. What is the name of the Christmas book that Charles Dickens wrote a year after *A Christmas Carol*?

2. The classic Christmas movie *Miracle on 34th Street* has been made twice. Can you name both years of release?

3. George Bailey has four children in *It's A Wonderful Life*. What are their names?

4. In *National Lampoon's Christmas Vacation*, what is the name of Ellen's cousin's husband?

5. What actress played Susan in the original *Miracle on 34th Street*?

6. What animated movie includes the characters Heat Miser and Snow Miser?

7. What is the name of Tiny Tim's oldest sister in *A Christmas Carol*?

8. What is Santa's full name in *Bad Santa*?

9. Which actor played Scrooge in the 1970 movie *Scrooge*?

10. Which actor played Frank Cross in the 1988 movie *Scrooged*?

**11.** Which actor played Scrooge in the 1951 adaptation of *A Christmas Carol* called *Scrooge*?

**12.** Which actor voiced Scrooge in the 1992 movie *The Muppet Christmas Carol*?

**13.** Which actor played Scrooge in the 1984 version of *A Christmas Carol*?

**14.** What age is Kevin McCallister in *Home Alone*?

**15.** Which actor played Kate McCallister in *Home Alone*?

# Quiz 28

## Christmas Mix

**1.** What does Harry Potter receive as a Christmas present from the Weasleys for his first Christmas at Hogwarts?

**2.** In *Frozen* Elsa creates a giant white snowman. What is its name?

**3.** **Fill in the blank:** Complete the book title written by Dougie Poynter and Tom Fletcher, *The Dinosaur that _____ Christmas.*

**4.** In *The Snowman*, where do the snowman and the boy go walking?
   **a** In the air
   **b** In the pub
   **c** In the street
   **d** In the town

**5.** Which pantomime features two ugly sisters who treat the heroine badly?

**6.** Three of Santa's reindeer have names beginning with a D. What are their names?

**7.** What noisy object do elves traditionally have on their shoes?

**8.** What is the name of the boy in the book *The Christmas Pig*?

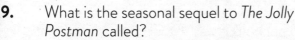

**9.** What is the seasonal sequel to *The Jolly Postman* called?
   **a**  *The Jolly Postman at Christmas*
   **b**  *The Jolly Postman Loves Christmas*
   **c**  *The Jolly Christmas Postman*
   **d**  *The Jolly Postman's Christmas Adventure*

**10.** Which of the following is a common gift to fill a Christmas stocking?
   **a**  A 50 pence piece
   **b**  A penny
   **c**  Penny sweets
   **d**  Chocolate coins

**11.** What popular carol involves a different gift every day leading up to Christmas?

**12.** **True or false?** In Edwardian times a pig's head was a popular Christmas meal.

**13.** In which selection box would you find a Toffee Finger?

**14.** What movie features the quote 'Merry Christmas you filthy animal'?

**15.** **True or false?** Christmas crackers are illegal after Boxing Day.

## Christmas Mix

**1.** What colour was the Christmas Elvis spent without 'you'?

**2.** How many Christmases are there in the title of the Reese Witherspoon and Vince Vaughn movie from 2008?

**3.** **Fill in the blank:** Complete the line from *The Lion, The Witch and The Wardrobe*, 'Always winter but never _____'.

**4.** Which *Friends* cast member attended 2016's *Office Christmas Party*?

**5.** In *It's A Wonderful Life*, what is the full name of the guardian angel?

**6.** Which actor became *Doctor Who* in a 2005 episode entitled 'The Christmas Invasion'?

**7.** When do the 'twelve days of Christmas' start?

**8.** Which member of *The Simpsons* delivered the Channel 4 alternative Christmas message in 2004?
- **a** Mr Burns
- **b** Homer
- **c** Maggie
- **d** Marge

**9.** Can you name the Grinch's dog?

**10.** In what book do the characters set sail from Nantucket on Christmas Day?

**11.** Which actress co-wrote the film *Last Christmas*?

**12.** In the movie *Elf*, Buddy lives by the Code of the Elves. What is the first rule in the code?

**13.** Gavin and Stacey returned to TV for a Christmas special in 2019. How many years had it been off-air before the reunion?

**14.** In *Mean Girls*, which Christmas song do The Plastics perform on stage?

**15.** Who plays the part of the Angel in the 2020 movie *Christmas on the Square*?

Answers on page 294

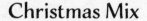

## Christmas Mix

**1.** In *Downton Abbey*, which character died in a car accident in the 2012 Christmas special?

**2.** What singer released the album *Christmas in the Heart*?

**3.** When was the movie *The Holiday* released?

**4.** In England they are pigs in blankets. What are they called in Scotland?

**5.** In *Love Actually*, what boy band does Billy Mack beat to get his Christmas number one?

**6.** What Christmas song plays at the end of *Die Hard*?

**7.** In what year was the first charity Christmas card sent in aid of UNICEF?

**8.** Who plays the part of Jeronicus Jangle in *Jingle Jangle*?

**9.** What year was the first Christmas special of *Death in Paradise* broadcast in the UK?

**10.** What was finally dissolved over Christmas in 1991?

**11.** In *About A Boy*, Hugh Grant's character receives royalties from a song his father wrote. Can you name the song?

**12.** Who composed the music that can be heard at the beginning of *Frozen*?

**13.** What name is given to an adult male turkey?

**14.** What is the name of Scrooge's fiancée in *A Christmas Carol*?

**15.** What are the names of the two baddies in *Home Alone*?

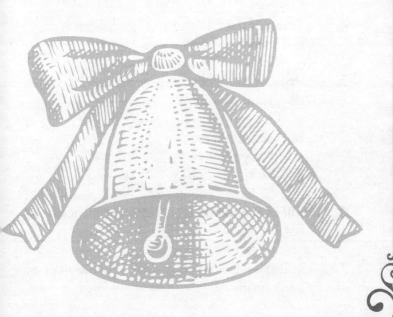

# Quiz 29

## Christmas in the British Isles

1. Which meat is most commonly served for Christmas dinner in England?
   a Beef
   b Chicken
   c Goose
   d Turkey

2. **True or false?** For there to be an 'official' white Christmas in the UK, only one snowflake has to land on Christmas Day.

3. Does the Welsh tradition of *Plygain* take place on Christmas Day or New Year's Day?

4. **True or false?** The Queen's Christmas Broadcast is live every year.

5. What is the official day to put up Christmas decorations in England?
   a 1 December
   b 12 December
   c 24 December
   d There isn't one

6. **Fill in the blank:** Complete the famous ballet title, *Swan* _____ .

7. In England, which two days in December are bank holidays?

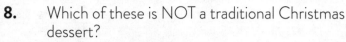

**8.** Which of these is NOT a traditional Christmas dessert?
   **a** Christmas cake
   **b** Christmas pudding
   **c** Sticky toffee pudding
   **d** Yule log

**9.** As of January 2022, who has had the most Christmas number ones, The Beatles or LadBaby?

**10.** **True or false?** A Christmas morning running race is held every year in Porthcawl, Wales.

**11.** What does Harry Potter receive as a Christmas present from the Dursleys for his first Christmas at Hogwarts?

**12.** What do the actors often throw at the audience during a pantomime?

**13.** In 2021, Sylvia Pope became a Guinness World Record holder. What for?
   **a** The biggest turkey
   **b** The longest tinsel
   **c** The most Christmas trees
   **d** The most festive ornaments

**14.** What retail tradition starts on Boxing Day?

**15.** In the pantomime *Jack and the Beanstalk*, what does Jack trade for magic beans?

# Christmas in the British Isles

1. Where would you find an ashen faggot in the UK?
   a East Anglia
   b South West of England
   c Scotland
   d Wales

2. What is the name of the cake that used to be commonly sold and eaten after Christmas in England?

3. Traditionally, when does Harrods open its Christmas department: July, August or September?

4. **True or false?** In Wales, the blood bowl is a decorative bowl that is often passed around at Christmas.

5. What year was the first *Only Fools and Horses* Christmas special aired?

6. Where in the UK might you hear *Blythe Yule*?

7. What was made on *Noson Gyflaith*, a traditional festivity in some areas of north Wales?

8. Traditionally, how many plums do you put in plum pudding at Christmas?

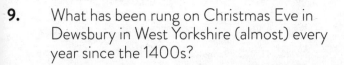

**9.** What has been rung on Christmas Eve in Dewsbury in West Yorkshire (almost) every year since the 1400s?

**10.** In which country would you say *Nadolig Llawen*?

**11.** What was depicted on the first official Christmas card to be sent in England?

**12.** What year saw the release of two of the most popular Christmas songs, 'Do They Know It's Christmas?' and 'Last Christmas'?

**13.** **True or false?** The origins of pantomime are linked to the Italian *commedia dell'arte*.

**14.** On what date did London-born Charlie Chaplin die?

**15.** Where in the UK might you hear *Blythe Yuletide*?

Answers on page 297

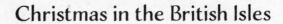

## Christmas in the British Isles

**1.** Scottish students stole something from Westminster Abbey on Christmas Day in 1950. What was it?

**2.** What is the key ingredient of stargazey pie?

**3.** According to the Met Office, only one of the following was a white Christmas in the UK; 2018, 2019 or 2020. Which was it?

**4.** In Wales *pwnco* accompanies the folk custom *Mari Lwyd*. Is it an exchange of presents, food or rhymes?

**5.** In what year did Boxing Day become a national holiday in Scotland?

**6.** What name is given to the songs that are sung in packed pubs in Yorkshire at Christmas?

**7.** Where in the UK would you say *Nadelik Lowen*?

**8.** How long is the traditional Welsh *Nos Galan* road race, held annually on New Year's Eve?

**9.** What is the Welsh name for Santa Claus?

**10.** Popular on the Isle of Man, what is *jough y nollick*?

**11.** Why might some Irish households light a candle in their window on Christmas Eve?

**12.** What is carried through Allendale, Northumberland during Tar Bar'l on New Year's Eve?

**13.** Stir-up Sunday is traditionally the last Sunday before what?

**14.** According to a YouGov poll in 2017, what was the UK's favourite Quality Street chocolate?

**15.** And what was the UK's least favourite Quality Street chocolate?

## Yuletide

1. What plant with white berries was sacred to Celts, Norse people and Native Americans and is often hung for a kiss?

2. **True or false?** It was a Roman tradition to eat Christmas pudding on Christmas Day.

3. What did Romans do at Christmas time that is very similar to modern traditions?
   a They dressed up as Santa
   b They exchanged gifts
   c They hung up stockings on Christmas Eve
   d They went carol singing

4. During the winter solstice, either of the Earth's poles are at maximum tilt from what?

5. **True or false?** People worshipped silently during the winter solstice.

6. **Fill in the blank:** In many parts of Europe, a Yule _____ is burned at Christmas.

7. Where did the tradition of wassailing originate?
   a Anglo-Saxons
   b Celts
   c Greeks
   d Romans

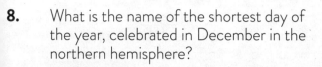

**8.** What is the name of the shortest day of the year, celebrated in December in the northern hemisphere?

**9.** **True or false?** Christmas is a Roman word.

**10.** Which of the following words is derived from Old Norse?
   **a** Nativity
   **b** Noel
   **c** Xmas
   **d** Yule

**11.** What would you do at a Norwegian *julebord*?

**12.** What is a Smoking Bishop: food or a drink?

**13.** **Fill in the blank:** An old tradition was to eat one _____ pie every day for the twelve days of Christmas.

**14.** **True or false?** Victorian children would attend boxing matches on Boxing Day.

**15.** What is *Julebukking*, a Scandinavian Christmas tradition?
   **a** Going door to door singing
   **b** Cutting a yule log
   **c** Baking a yule log
   **d** Dressing up as Father Christmas

# Quiz 30

## Yuletide

1. Romans displayed wreaths during a festival which began on 17 December. What were they often made from?
   a  Holly
   b  Glass
   c  Mistletoe
   d  Tinsel

2. What name is given to the Celtic equivalent of a priest?

3. In Norse mythology, which god is said to have travelled to Earth disguised in a cloak leaving gifts of bread?

4. **True or false?** Wassailing has its roots in a Pagan custom of visiting wheat fields to sing and ensure a good harvest.

5. In the USA, what drink is traditionally served to carol singers?

6. **True or false?** The winter solstice always falls on New Year's Eve.

7. How many legs did Odin's horse have?

8. What was burned in ancient times to represent the reborn sun?

**9.** What is the Old English word for yule?
  **a** *Yul*
  **b** *Jol*
  **c** *Gēol*
  **d** *Gole*

**10.** What popular Christmas drink is similar to the wassail drink?

**11.** During the winter solstice what celestial being did the Romans worship?

**12.** In Norse mythology the *álfar*, or 'hidden people', evolved into what contemporary part of our Christmas story?

**13.** These days Father Christmas wears red and white, but in the past what was a more common colour for his clothes?

**14.** Which is the odd one out?
  **a** Egghot
  **b** Lambswool
  **c** Whipcoll
  **d** Koolwhip

**15.** How long did the ancient festival of Yule last?

Answers on page 300

# Yuletide

**1.** What is the name of the Roman festival that took place in December and included partying, gift-giving and feasting?

**2.** Which Roman god is associated with ivy?

**3.** When you are wassailing, what would you hope to be served a drink from?

**4.** What is the traditional season for mummers, folk plays, in England?

**5.** What was the name of Odin's horse?

**6.** *Lohri* is a winter festival from which country?

**7.** An ancient British tradition at Christmas involved the Lord of what?

**8.** In Norse mythology, what is the name of Odin's son?

**9.** What language does the word solstice originate from?

**10.** The Anglo-Saxon phrase *wæs hæl* has become what contemporary word?

**11.** In Norse mythology, what was used to kill Odin's son?

**12.** Rounded to the nearest hour, how much shorter is the day in London during the winter solstice compared to the summer solstice?

**13.** In what year (to the nearest 10) did the church in Rome designate 25 December as Christ's birth date?

**14.** In Medieval times, what was the word for a dance with singing that could celebrate any festival?

**15.** What is the traditional date to go wassailing?

# General Knowledge

1. What is the name of Kristoff's reindeer in *Frozen*?

2. **Fill in the blank:** Complete the name of the pantomime, *Dick* _____ .

3. In which Christmas movie does Tom Hanks play six of the characters?

4. Who says 'God bless us, every one!' at the end of *A Christmas Carol*?

5. Which of the Wise Men's gifts begins with M?

6. **Fill in the blank:** Complete the Cadbury Roses chocolate, Strawberry _____ .

7. In what kingdom does Anna live in *Frozen*?

8. In *Harry Potter and the Goblet of Fire*, the Yule Ball is part of which event?

9. In *The Santa Clause*, what happens to Scott Calvin as he turns into Santa?
   a  He starts to speak Norwegian
   b  He grows a beard
   c  He can only say, 'Ho ho ho!'
   d  He magically flies

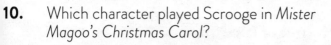

**10.** Which character played Scrooge in *Mister Magoo's Christmas Carol*?

**11.** **Fill in the blank:** Complete the carol title, 'Joy to the _____'.

**12.** In Croatia who leaves presents for children on 6 December: Saint Nicholas or Saint Catherine?

**13.** What colour is the Snowman's scarf in *The Snowman*?

**14.** On the first day of Christmas, where was the partridge?

**15.** **True or false?** There is a Cadbury Creme Egg in a box of Celebrations.

# General Knowledge

1. **True or false?** The movie *Last Christmas* features music by George Michael and Wham!.

2. **Fill in the blank:** Complete the opening sentence of Little Women, 'Christmas won't be Christmas without any _____'.

3. Who played the part of Hercule Poirot in 'Hercule Poirot's Christmas', first broadcast in the UK in 1994?

4. **Fill in the blank:** Complete the title of this anthology, *Afraid of the _____ Lights*.

5. Which television show had a two-part Christmas special as its finale, in which Tim and Dawn finally get together?

6. In *Enemy of the State* who plays Bobby Dean, out Christmas shopping before his world is turned upside-down?

7. Who proposes to Nessa in the *Gavin and Stacey* Christmas special of 2008?

8. **True or false?** Singer Ricky Martin voices a character in *Jingle Bells*.

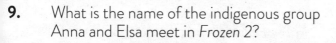

**9.** What is the name of the indigenous group Anna and Elsa meet in *Frozen 2*?

**10.** In the movie *Elf*, director Jon Favreau appears on screen. Who does he play?

**11.** **Fill in the blank:** Name Kevin's neighbour in *Home Alone*, Old Man _____ .

**12.** In 2014 in Angel Stadium Anaheim, USA, 30,333 people made a new record for wearing an article of clothing. What was it?

**13.** How many types of chocolate are included in Cadbury Roses selection boxes?

**14.** In the pantomime Aladdin, what is the occupation of Widow Twankey?

**15.** **True or false?** Donald Trump makes a cameo appearance in *Home Alone*.

Answers on page 303

# General Knowledge

**1.** In *The Holiday*, what is Iris's job?

**2.** Who starred in both *Game of Thrones* and *Last Christmas*?

**3.** What is the name of the shop in *Jingle Jangle*?

**4.** What are the names of the central couple in *Four Christmases*?

**5.** Which two Academy Awards® was *Home Alone* nominated for?

**6.** Christmas is mentioned in two of Shakespeare's plays. Can you name them?

**7.** What is the name of Scrooge's first employer in *A Christmas Carol*?

**8.** Leonard Bernstein gave a concert in Berlin on Christmas Day in 1989. What did the orchestra play?

**9.** In what year was Christmas banned in England?

**10.** In what pantomime would you find the character Carabosse?

**11.** What channel broadcast *A Boy Called Christmas* in the UK in 2021?

**12.** According to a 2019 YouGov poll, what was the most popular Christmas sweet treat?

**13.** In what year was *Klaus* nominated for the Best Animated Feature at the Academy Awards®?

**14.** In Bulgaria, Father Christmas is known as *Dyado Koleda*, which literally means what?

**15.** Who does Scrooge spend Christmas afternoon with in *A Christmas Carol*?

Answers on page 304

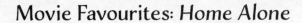

# Quiz 32

## Movie Favourites: Home Alone

1. In what city does Kevin live in *Home Alone*?

2. **Fill in the blank:** Name the actor that played Kevin, Macaulay _____ .

3. What is the name of Kevin's oldest brother?

4. In *Home Alone* what does Kevin wish for the night before his family holiday?

5. In *Home Alone 2* where does Kevin fly to?

6. What hotel does Kevin stay at in *Home Alone 2*?
   a The Hilton
   b The Standard
   c The Plaza
   d Waldorf Astoria

7. Where are Kevin's family heading for Christmas in *Home Alone 2*?

8. What birds feature prominently in *Home Alone 2*?

9. **True or false?** Macaulay Culkin stars in *Home Alone 3*.

10. How old was Macaulay Culkin during *Home Alone*?

**11.** What year was *Home Alone* released?
    **a** 1989
    **b** 1990
    **c** 1991
    **d** 1992

**12.** **True or false?** *Home Alone 4* was released in cinemas in 2002.

**13.** What is the name of Macaulay Culkin's brother, who also appeared in *Home Alone*?

**14.** Can you name the latest movie in the *Home Alone* franchise, released in 2021?

**15.** How many years after *Home Alone* is *Home Alone 2* set?

Answers on page 305

# Movie Favourites: *Love Actually*

**1.** Where does *Love Actually* begin and end?

**2.** What is the name of Billy Mack's manager?

**3.** What song is played at Juliet and Peter's wedding?

**4.** Who is Jamie's girlfriend having an affair with?

**5.** What shape is the necklace Harry buys for Mia?

**6.** What gift does Harry buy for his wife Karen?

**7.** What do *Love Actually* and *Bad Santa* have in common?

**8.** What was the name of Daniel's wife?

**9.** Who plays the part of Carol, the mother of Sam's friend Joanna?

**10.** Where does Colin go in the USA?

**11.** What are the names of the characters played by Martin Freeman and Joanna Page?

**12.** What is the name of Sarah's brother?

**13.** What is the name of the Creative Director where Sarah works?

**14.** What is the name of the character played by Rowan Atkinson?

**15.** Who directed *Love Actually*?

# Movie Favourites: Love Actually

**1.** What two characters are not linked to the others in any way?

**2.** What are the names of the three American girls Colin meets in the bar?

**3.** Who wrote *Love Actually*?

**4.** To what song does Hugh Grant's Prime Minister dance around 10 Downing Street?

**5.** Where does most of the manuscript to Jamie's novel end up?

**6.** What real world event is mentioned briefly in the movie?

**7.** In what year was *Love Actually* released?

**8.** What make of car does Colin Firth's character drive?

**9.** What is written on the sign on Sam's door?

**10.** **Fill in the blank:** Billy Mack describes his manager as 'The _____ _____ in the world'.

**11.** What does Sarah get her brother for Christmas?

**12.** Which female actor from *Rising Damp* was cut from the movie?

**13.** What is John and Judy's job?

**14.** What famous French actress is seen getting into a cab at Marseille airport?

**15.** Where were the 10 Downing Street scenes filmed?

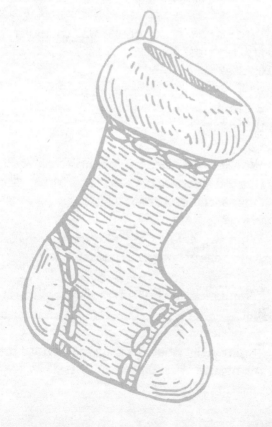

## Tick Tock

Time yourself to see how many questions you can get right in five minutes!

**1.** How many reindeer does Father Christmas have pulling his sleigh?

**2.** **Fill in the blank:** On Christmas Eve children often leave this sweet treat out for Father Christmas: _____ pies.

**3.** What is the most popular way to cook turkey at Christmas?
   **a** Bake it
   **b** Fry it
   **c** Roast it
   **d** Steam it

**4.** What movie, released at Christmas 2021, was the Academy Award® winner for Best Animated Feature in 2022?

**5.** What two colours most commonly make up a candy cane?

**6.** What colour is the trim on Father Christmas's suit?

**7.** Traditionally what is a snowman's nose made from?

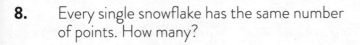

**8.** Every single snowflake has the same number of points. How many?

**9.** What three words follow 'O Come All Ye Faithful' in the famous carol?
  **a** Joyful and triumphant
  **b** Joyful and stuffed
  **c** Happy and winning
  **d** Merry and bright

**10.** What might you open every day in the days leading up to Christmas?

**11.** What (sometimes unpopular) green vegetable is commonly served at Christmas?

**12.** **Fill in the blank:** Complete the pantomime title, _____ *White and the* _____
  _____ .

**13.** Which of the following would you NOT use to decorate a Christmas tree?
  **a** Baubles
  **b** A fairy
  **c** A wreath
  **d** Tinsel

**14.** **True or false?** Santa has a reindeer named Thunderflash.

**15.** In the song, how many ships come sailing in on Christmas Day in the morning?

Answers on page 308

## Tick Tock

Time yourself to see how many questions you can get right in four minutes!

1. What is the title of the song in which chestnuts are roasting on an open fire?

2. What do you traditionally find in the middle of a stollen?

3. **Fill in the blank:** According to the 1944 song, 'All I Want For Christmas (Is My _____ _____ _____ )'.

4. In which pantomime would you find Wishee-Washee?

5. How many sizes too small was the Grinch's heart?

6. What is the name of the character played by Denise Richards in *The World is Not Enough*?

7. What is The Goons' song released in 1956 with Christmas in the title?

8. Who plays Lieutenant Colonel John Lawrence in *Merry Christmas, Mr. Lawrence*?

9. Which actor plays Howard Langston in *Jingle All The Way*?

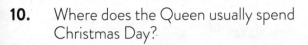

**10.** Where does the Queen usually spend Christmas Day?

**11.** Which band had the last UK number one of the twentieth century?

**12.** Who sang the first line of 'Do They Know It's Christmas?' in 1984?

**13.** Who starred in the 1996 movie *Santa With Muscles*?

**14.** Which country celebrates Christmas in summer: Peru, Venezuela or Guyana?

**15.** What song is playing as the characters dance and celebrate at the end of *The Holiday*?

## Tick Tock

Time yourself to see how many questions you can get right in three minutes!

**1.** What Disney character is always on television in Sweden on Christmas Eve?

**2.** Who played Kris Kringle in the 1994 version of *Miracle on 34th Street*?

**3.** In 1986 what did the band Half Man Half Biscuit want for Christmas?

**4.** Who banned Christmas first, England or Scotland?

**5.** Disney released a new animated movie on Christmas Day in 1963 in the US. What was it called?

**6.** What is the English name for the popular Christmas plant known as *Viscum album*?

**7.** Good King Wenceslas was king of what country?

**8.** What is the name of the toy Howard Langston is trying to get hold of in *Jingle All The Way*?

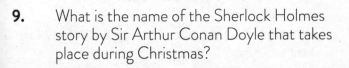

**9.** What is the name of the Sherlock Holmes story by Sir Arthur Conan Doyle that takes place during Christmas?

**10.** In what country would you be if you were eating *pepparkakor* at Christmas?

**11.** What is the name of the fourth Christmas single released by The Killers in 2009?

**12.** Who wrote *The Mistletoe Murder and Other Stories*?

**13.** In what year were the first Christmas stamps issued in the UK?

**14.** What was the title of William Shatner's Christmas album, released in 2018?

**15.** The character Alfred Jingle appears in which famous book by Charles Dickens?

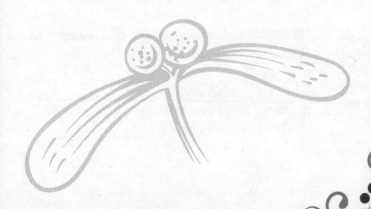

Answers on page 310

# Happy New Year

1. What is the name given to the day before New Year's Day in England?

2. The Roman God Janus was associated with which month of the year?

3. What loud, colourful explosives are used to see in the new year all over the world?

4. Which door of your house should you open to 'let the old year out'; the front door or the back door?

5. What song is traditionally sung at midnight on New Year's Eve?

6. **True or false?** In Scotland, New Year's Eve celebration is known as Hogmanay.

7. What is the most famous bell that strikes midnight in the UK on New Year's Eve?

8. What do many people make on 1 January to start the new year?
   a  New Year's Cakes
   b  New Year's Crafts
   c  New Year's Revelations
   d  New Year's Resolutions

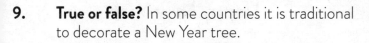

**9.** **True or false?** In some countries it is traditional to decorate a New Year tree.

**10.** What do people jump off at New Year in Denmark so they can 'leap into the new year'?
   **a** A bed
   **b** A chair
   **c** A ladder
   **d** The kitchen table

**11.** **True or false?** New Year's Eve is a bank holiday in England.

**12.** In Scotland, what should you carry with you on New Year's Eve to bring luck: coal, chalk or cheese?

**13.** What is it common to do on New Year's Day in Whitley Bay, Scarborough and the Firth of Forth?

**14.** **True or false?** The traditional New Year's Day meal is fish and chips.

**15.** Where do New Yorkers famously gather on New Year's Eve?

## Happy New Year

1. What day of the week was New Year's Day in 2022?
   a Friday
   b Saturday
   c Sunday
   d Monday

2. How many grapes should you eat in Spain if you want a happy new year?

3. Where would you be if you heard Queen Margrethe II deliver a speech on New Year's Eve?

4. What is the Scottish New Year tradition of visiting others known as?

5. In Ireland what is traditionally used to bang against doors and walls of your home at new year?
   a Apples
   b Bread
   c Potatoes
   d Oats

6. In Stonehaven, Scotland, what flaming objects are paraded through the streets at New Year?

7. Which country had great success in 2021, with nationals winning UEFA Euro 2020, The Great British Bake Off and Eurovision?

8. In Scotland what are the first two bank holidays of the year?

9. In Whittlesea, what is made of straw for a parade in January each year?

10. What giant object is dropped in Times Square to signal the new year?

11. What calendar, proposed by Julius Caesar, replaced the Roman calendar?

12. What do J. Edgar Hoover, Christine Lagarde and Grandmaster Flash have in common?

13. In 1999 a huge computer meltdown was predicted. What was it called?

14. Who wrote 'Auld Lang Syne'?

15. In China 2022 is the year of which animal?

# Happy New Year

1. In Brazil it is a tradition to jump into what at new year?
   a A cake
   b The sea
   c Your home
   d Your lover's arms

2. In what language does *Blwydden Newydd Dda* mean Happy New Year?

3. What does 'Auld Lang Syne' mean when literally translated?

4. In Scotland, what is commonly eaten on New Year's Day?

5. In Wales, what is *calennig*?
   a New Year's cake
   b New Year's gift
   c New Year's song
   d New Year's trick

6. In Scottish tradition, it brings luck if what sort of man comes into your house after midnight on New Year's Eve?

7. In Greece what is traditionally hung up in doorways at New Year?

**8.** In Germany what metal is poured into water at New Year to predict fortunes?

**9.** In what country are *oliebollen* common at New Year?

**10.** In Colombia it is a New Year tradition to carry what object to encourage travel in the coming year?

**11.** What took over from the Julian calendar in 1582?

**12.** What newspaper was published for the first time on 1 January 1785?

**13.** What political body came into being on New Year's Day in 1958?

**14.** In American college football, what name is given to the game traditionally played on New Year's Day?

**15.** Which island nation rings in New Year before anyone else?

# Answers

## Quiz 1:
## General Knowledge

1.  True
2.  A
3.  Claus
4.  Christmas Day
5.  A star
6.  Boxing Day
7.  Queen Elizabeth II
8.  Sing, 'Hark the Herald Angels Sing'
9.  Wrap them up
10. False, he was a reindeer
11. *Nightmare*
12. D
13. 12
14. A paper crown
15. Kiss

# Answers

## Quiz 1:
## General Knowledge

1. True

2. A

3. Saint Nicholas

4. Happy New Year

5. Gold

6. False

7. C

8. Gentlemen

9. C

10. Vixen

11. *Home Alone*

12. False, Norway does

13. Sausage rolls

14. A

15. Santa Claus

## Quiz 1:
## General Knowledge

1.  Lebkuchen
2.  Wassailing
3.  Lapland
4.  Cranberry sauce
5.  Balthasar, Caspar (Gaspar), Melchior
6.  D
7.  Nazareth
8.  Wenceslas
9.  Christmas Eve
10. 'Jingle Bells' aboard the *Gemini 6*
11. Jason Statham
12. Oxford Street
13. 1980
14. 'Silent Night'
15. Xbox 360

1. B
2. Snow
3. The Grinch
4. True, he has had three
5. *Princess*
6. C
7. Christmas
8. *The Voice*
9. B ('Postman Pat's Magic Christmas')
10. *The Gruffalo*
11. True
12. Shaun the Sheep
13. Mice
14. A
15. The Simpsons

## Quiz 2:
## Christmas TV

1. 2005

2. D

3. Girls Aloud

4. Battersea

5. C

6. False, it was 'Merry Christmas Mr. Bean'

7. Roasting

8. *A Christmas Carol* by Charles Dickens

9. Armadillo

10. False

11. 'Knowing Me, Knowing Yule with Alan Partridge'

12. C

13. 2004

14. The Queen Vic

15. D

## Quiz 2:
## ChristmasTV

1. 1977
2. Poo
3. The Snowmen
4. The Waltons
5. *Spitting Image*
6. *The Office*
7. 'In Excelsis Deo'
8. Greyhound
9. *Lost*
10. Christmas Eve
11. She goes into labour
12. 'Holy'
13. Three
14. 'My Own Personal Jesus'
15. 1997

## Quiz 3:
## Christmas Number Ones

1. LadBaby
2. 'Do They Know It's Christmas?'
3. Child
4. Rage Against the Machine
5. True
6. C
7. True
8. Elton John and Ed Sheeran
9. Military Wives
10. Michael Jackson
11. Brother
12. True
13. C
14. Clean Bandit
15. Sausage rolls

# Answers

## Quiz 3:
## Christmas Number Ones

1.  Wings

2.  Wine

3.  Green ('Green, Green Grass of Home')

4.  B

5.  Liverpool

6.  Everybody

7.  Ed Sheeran

8.  '2 Become 1', 'Too Much', 'Goodbye'

9.  'Hallelujah'

10. Mud

11. False, they did with 'Another Brick in the Wall (Part 2)'

12. Nicole Kidman

13. 'When We Collide'

14. 'A Bridge Over You'

15. C

## Quiz 3:
## Christmas Number Ones

1. 'These Are the Days of Our Lives'

2. 'Soleado'

3. 'Hello, Goodbye'

4. 1962

5. 1952

6. 'Mary's Boy Child / Oh My Lord'

7. 'Bohemian Rhapsody' by Queen

8. LadBaby

9. 'Skyscraper'

10. Four (One with The Shadows, two solo, one with Band Aid 20)

11. The Beatles

12. Friday (Christmas Day)

13. 'Do They Know It's Christmas' by Band Aid

14. The Trussell Trust

15. 'Moon River'

# Answers

## Quiz 4:
## Christmas Carols

1. Three
2. Boughs of holly
3. A partridge in a pear tree
4. False
5. Ding Dong
6. Ivy
7. (Little lord) Jesus
8. On the feast of Stephen
9. Bethlehem
10. Night
11. False
12. Watched their flocks
13. D
14. Faithful
15. D

## Quiz 4:
## Christmas Carols

1. The USA
2. Christina Rossetti
3. 'God Rest Ye Merry Gentlemen'
4. World
5. 'The Little Drummer Boy'
6. Dusty
7. 'Peace On Earth'
8. False, it was written in 1962
9. 1649
10. Wales
11. The birth of Christ
12. True
13. Snow
14. Crib
15. Midnight

# Answers

## Quiz 4:
## Christmas Carols

1. Handel's *Messiah*
2. 'Silent Night' ('Stille Nacht')
3. Latin
4. Charles Wesley
5. A lowly cattle shed
6. In sweet rejoicing
7. Bethlehem
8. The 'Coventry Carol'
9. 364
10. Figgy pudding
11. 'Up On The Housetop'
12. Wenceslaus I, Duke of Bohemia
13. Three French hens (two turtle doves and a partridge in a pear tree)
14. Cecil Frances Alexander
15. 1880 (in Truro, Cornwall)

## Quiz 5:
## Christmas Movies

1. Santa/Elves
2. *Christmas*
3. Father Christmas
4. None
5. *A Christmas Carol*
6. Eleanor Fay Bloomingbottom
7. Cornwall
8. Santa Claus
9. Belgravia and Montenaro
10. Tom Hanks
11. D
12. *The Snowman*
13. Scissorhands
14. Prince Richard
15. Arnold Schwarzenegger

# Answers

## Quiz 5:
## Christmas Movies

1. *It's A Wonderful Life*
2. *Holiday Inn*
3. D
4. Judy Garland
5. Los Angeles International Airport
6. Charles Dickens
7. *Bad Santa*
8. Michael Caine
9. Billy Mack
10. Laurel and Hardy
11. Renée Zellweger
12. Danny DeVito
13. D
14. Ron Howard
15. Six

## Quiz 5:
## Christmas Movies

1. *A Very Harold & Kumar Christmas*

2. Oswald Cobblepot

3. Nell and Simon

4. Cameron Diaz

5. *Holiday Inn*

6. Clark W. Griswold, Jr.

7. Feed it after midnight

8. Fred Astaire

9. *Last Christmas*

10. Zenotek

11. Chicago Transit Authority

12. 'Have Yourself A Merry Little Christmas'

13. Frank Capra

14. Isaac Greenberg

15. Edmund Gwenn

# Answers

## Quiz 6:
## Christmas Adverts

1. An alien

2. B

3. A chimney

4. 'Rocking Around the Christmas Tree'

5. Percy Pig

6. A stepdad

7. Ice skates

8. A trampoline

9. A

10. 'Magic Moments'

11. Moon

12. 1914

13. Yellow Pages

14. Sainsbury's

15. False, it was Elton John

# Answers

## Quiz 6:
## Christmas Adverts

1. Oxo
2. Woolworths (and Woolco!)
3. Gives his parents a present
4. B
5. Penguin
6. Corn Flakes
7. Lorry
8. Marks & Spencer
9. Irn Bru
10. Boots
11. Lily Allen
12. D
13. TK Maxx
14. JD Sports
15. Boots

# Answers

## Quiz 6:
## Christmas Adverts

1. Amazon
2. House of Fraser
3. Selfridges
4. Sports Direct
5. Lurpak butter
6. Aliens
7. Mrs Claus
8. Kevin
9. Sainsbury's
10. McDonald's
11. Disney
12. Taika Waititi
13. Robin
14. Bears
15. Wes Anderson

## Quiz 7:
## General Knowledge

1. *A Christmas Prince: The Royal Wedding*

2. False

3. 24 December (Christmas Eve)

4. Stocking

5. Beanstalk

6. Ebeneezer Scrooge

7. Sausage

8. D

9. True

10. *The Santa Clause 2*

11. Mother Goose

12. Savoury

13. True

14. 12

15. Father Christmas

# Answers

## Quiz 7:
## General Knowledge

1.   'Last Christmas' by Wham!

2.   Puerto Rican

3.   *Strictly Come Dancing*

4.   False, he was dressed as Lady Diana Spencer

5.   'Christmas Is All Around'

6.   Take That

7.   His tongue

8.   Saint Nicholas

9.   A candle

10.   The Statue of Liberty

11.   Russia

12.   Christ's mass

13.   Christmas Eve

14.   1,200 years

15.   Red

## Quiz 7:
## General Knowledge

1. Macy's
2. 1660
3. 'Everything She Wants'
4. 1843
5. 8 December
6. Salted cod
7. 7 January
8. Trifle
9. 'O Come All Ye Faithful'
10. Befana
11. For Britain's support in World War II
12. Seven-pointed star
13. Merry Christmas in Gaelic
14. New Zealand
15. Henry Travers

# Answers

## Quiz 8:
## Christmas Toys

1. Sylvanian Families
2. Batmobile
3. False, it was black and white
4. D
5. 'Beyond'
6. False
7. 'Yes we can!'
8. Xbox 360
9. Nintendo
10. *High School Musical*
11. B
12. Red
13. *Frozen*
14. Blue
15. False, it's a bicycle

## Quiz 8:
## Christmas Toys

1. Ghosts from *Ghostbusters*

2. *Ninja Turtles*

3. Tracy Island

4. POGs

5. *Who Wants To Be A Millionaire?*

6. Bratz

7. BeyBlades

8. PSP (PlayStation Portable)

9. False, it was a hamster

10. C

11. *Star Wars*

12. C

13. True

14. Cabbage Patch Kids

15. Decepticons

## Quiz 8:
## Christmas Toys

1. Optimus Prime
2. Panini football stickers
3. Digital pet
4. 1998
5. Teksta
6. A red blanket
7. 2011
8. Furby Boom
9. Atari
10. D
11. Koosh ball
12. Nintendo Entertainment System
13. Beanie Babies
14. Pokémon
15. Baby Yoda or The Child or Grogu

# Answers

## Quiz 9:
## Top of the Pops Christmas Specials

1. C
2. The Beatles
3. Wish
4. False, it was two parts
5. B
6. Slade
7. Moon
8. D
9. False
10. A
11. Elton John and Ed Sheeran
12. 'Perfect'
13. 'Kiss My (Uh Oh)'
14. False
15. Sausage rolls

# Answers

## Quiz 9:
### *Top of the Pops Christmas Specials*

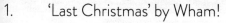

1.  'Last Christmas' by Wham!

2.  Slade and Wizzard

3.  C

4.  'Do They Know It's Christmas?' by Band Aid
    20 in 2004

5.  'Do They Know It's Christmas?' by Band Aid in
    1989

6.  True

7.  Mabel

8.  A

9.  Coldplay

10. Sigrid

11. Love

12. Glass Animals

13. 'Bad Habits' by Ed Sheeran

14. '(Call Me By Your Name)'

15. False, she had three

## Quiz 9:
### Top of the Pops Christmas Specials

1.  1973
2.  17
3.  Seven
4.  Westlife
5.  Wes Nelson
6.  'Mary's Boy Child' was a Christmas number one for both artists
7.  Three: 1984, 1989, 2004
8.  Womp
9.  Jess Glynne
10. Years & Years
11. Clara Amfo
12. 'Cake By The Ocean'
13. 2018
14. Four
15. 'When We Were Young'

# Answers

## Quiz 10:
## Christmas Celebrations

1. True
2. Nativity
3. Christmas tree
4. A
5. True
6. Goodwill/giving
7. Ivy
8. Pantomime
9. Sing carols
10. Bacon
11. A
12. False, mincemeat contains no meat
13. True
14. Advertisement
15. False, they are eaten at Easter

# Answers

## Quiz 10:
## Christmas Celebrations

1. Oliver Cromwell
2. D
3. True
4. A sixpence (or coin)
5. Whiskey
6. Tom Smith
7. Christmas Day
8. True
9. C
10. Blitzen
11. Orange juice
12. Twelfth Night (5 January)
13. False, it is usually a man
14. Christmas market
15. False

# Answers

## Quiz 10:
## Christmas Celebrations

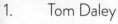

1.  Tom Daley

2.  1960

3.  Brandy

4.  2007

5.  Brandy or rum

6.  Brighton

7.  George V

8.  9 million

9.  Guatemala

10. Sprouts at 66 percent (broccoli was on 44 percent of plates)

11. A candle

12. 12

13. Milk, butter, onion, breadcrumbs, cloves, bay leaf

14. Poinsettia

15. 1974

# Answers

## Quiz 11:
## Father Christmas

1.   Santa Claus

2.   False

3.   A sleigh

4.   Reindeer

5.   Elves

6.   D

7.   True

8.   Down the chimney

9.   False, it is Saint Nick

10.  Ho ho ho!

11.  D

12.  Children

13.  False

14.  Send a letter

15.  B

# Answers

## Quiz 11:
## Father Christmas

1. "Twas the Night Before Christmas'

2. 1939

3. True, particularly in the USA

4. New York, USA

5. Mrs Claus

6. Nine

7. A lump of coal

8. False, it is HOH OHO

9. Carrot

10. *Père Noël*

11. To light the way with his nose

12. Coca-Cola

13. True

14. Twice

15. 'Santa Claus is Coming to Town'

# Answers

## Quiz 11:
## Father Christmas

1. Sailors
2. 'I Believe In Father Christmas'
3. NORAD (North American Aerospace Defense Command)
4. Colorado Springs, Colorado, USA
5. Turkey
6. ChristKind/Christkindl
7. Clement Clarke Moore
8. France (near Nancy)
9. 96930
10. 6 December
11. The Kinks
12. C
13. 'Boogie Woogie Santa Claus'
14. One-horse open sleigh
15. Eartha Kitt

## Quiz 12:
## Christmas Books

1. Stole it

2. Letters (*The Father Christmas Letters*)

3. Pig (*The Christmas Pig*)

4. *The Christmas Pine*

5. *Christmasaurus and the Naughty List*

6. Dogger (*Dogger's Christmas*)

7. Polar

8. Three

9. Two, a dog and a cat

10. *Little Women*

11. False, he can fly

12. C

13. False, it was called Greg

14. Christmas

15. D

# Answers

## Quiz 12:
## Christmas Books

1. Go on holiday (*Father Christmas Goes on Holiday*)
2. Bob Cratchit
3. Wales
4. O. Henry
5. *The Greatest Gift* by Philip Van Doren Stern
6. Cruella de Vil
7. *Eloise at Christmastime*
8. *The First Noel*
9. True
10. The Hogfather
11. *Terrors*
12. The Big Woods (*Christmas in the Big Woods*)
13. *The Dark is Rising*
14. *Delights*
15. *Gloucester*

## Quiz 12:
## Christmas Books

1. *Holidays on Ice*
2. *Christmas at Cold Comfort Farm*
3. L. Frank Baum
4. Simeon Lee
5. R.L. May
6. Rover (*Rover Saves Christmas*)
7. *The Stupidest Angel*
8. Tim Burton
9. *One More for Christmas*
10. *A Christmas Memory*
11. Cracker
12. Jack and Laurie
13. Cornwall
14. Dates (*The Twelve Dates of Christmas*)
15. 'Amazing Peace (A Christmas Poem)'

# Answers

## Quiz 13:
## General Knowledge

1. Blue

2. *Dick*

3. False, 'I Will Always Love You' in 1992

4. King Herod

5. Gobble

6. Paris

7. False, it's called *Diary of a Christmas Elf*

8. Tinsel

9. Bleak

10. Xmas

11. False, it's on Christmas Eve

12. Walter Hobbs

13. B

14. False, it is steamed

15. False

# Answers

## Quiz 13:
## General Knowledge

1.  True
2.  An air rifle (Red Ryder BB Gun)
3.  *Ghost Story*
4.  'He's behind you!'
5.  Grand Rapids, Michigan
6.  Professor Quirrell
7.  Cat
8.  6 January
9.  Odin
10. False, a game called Shoe the Wild Mare was popular
11. Holly
12. Yule Cat
13. True
14. 1933
15. Norway

# Answers

## Quiz 13:
## General Knowledge

1. Rudyard Kipling

2. Henry III

3. It burned in a fire

4. Australia

5. Sir Henry Cole

6. 1957

7. Poop (it literally means 'the pooper')

8. A whole almond

9. Straw

10. Other people's homes

11. They have antlers; male reindeer lose their antlers in winter

12. Bread

13. They were all born on 25 December

14. 24 December

15. A nativity scene

# Quiz 14:
# Christmas Around the World

1.  France (or Belgium)

2.  Christmas pudding

3.  False

4.  Spain

5.  Saint Nicholas

6.  Australia

7.  Denmark

8.  C

9.  A

10. B

11. True

12. Merry/Happy Christmas

13. Naples

14. Jamaica

15. False, there are two: 25 December and
    7 January

# Answers

## Quiz 14:
## Christmas Around the World

1.   Christmas Eve (24 December)

2.   Saint Lucia

3.   Gaelic

4.   C

5.   False, traditionally it is eaten on Christmas Eve

6.   The Netherlands

7.   China (it literally means Old Christmas Man)

8.   Denmark

9.   True

10.  White (with a red sash)

11.  B

12.  Greece

13.  True

14.  B

15.  Portugal and/or Brazil

# Answers

## Quiz 14:
## Christmas Around the World

1. Crib
2. Der Weihnachtsmann
3. Ireland
4. Nuremberg
5. 5 December
6. Apple
7. *Home For Christmas*
8. A sponge cake
9. Saffron buns
10. Finland
11. A type of bread in Greece, it means Christ's Bread
12. A bunch of twigs (for beating naughty children!)
13. Carols
14. Greece
15. Croatia

# Answers

## Quiz 15:
## Christmas Drinks

1.  False, it does

2.  D

3.  Chocolate

4.  Left (from an ancient naval tradition)

5.  False, there is a drink called *glögg*

6.  C

7.  No, there is a drink called Brandy Alexander

8.  False, you add hot water

9.  Rum

10. Hip flask

11. Winter Pimm's

12. Ireland

13. Brandy

14. Green

15. A polar bear

# Answers

## Quiz 15:
## Christmas Drinks

1. B
2. True
3. C
4. Bombardino
5. Digestif
6. True
7. Cream
8. True
9. *Frasier*
10. Wine (red then white)
11. C
12. Coffee
13. Orange
14. Moët & Chandon
15. Jack Daniels

# Answers

## Quiz 15:
## Christmas Drinks

1.  Punch

2.  Wassail bowl

3.  Whisky

4.  Wine and cider

5.  Raisins and almonds

6.  Smoking Bishop

7.  Ice cream

8.  Mimosa

9.  *Northwest Passage*

10. Hip flask

11. Warninks

12. D

13. Jamaica

14. Épernay, France

15. Heineken

# Answers

## Quiz 16:
## Festive Feasts

1.  Mince pies
2.  Holly (and Ivy)
3.  D
4.  Log
5.  Brussels sprouts
6.  Coca-Cola
7.  C
8.  False, it is popular in Poland
9.  Filo pastry
10. Chicken
11. Goose
12. No, it contains dried fruit
13. Saffron buns
14. D
15. Australia

# Answers

## Quiz 16:
## Festive Feasts

1.  Greece
2.  A sheep's head
3.  Seven
4.  Lamb (sometimes horse)
5.  Butter
6.  Stollen
7.  New Zealand
8.  Panettone
9.  B
10. C
11. Yule log, France
12. 12
13. True
14. Poland
15. False

# Answers

## Quiz 16:
## Festive Feasts

1. Russia
2. Narwhal
3. Rice pudding
4. China
5. *Rosca de Reyes* (Three Kings Cake)
6. Caraway seeds
7. Russia
8. Fruit cake
9. Sweden
10. Cod
11. Peru
12. Czech Republic
13. Finland
14. Scotland
15. Coquito

## Quiz 17:
## Christmas Decoration

1.    Baubles
2.    Stockings
3.    *Elf*
4.    C
5.    Wreath
6.    Christmas lights
7.    Evergreen
8.    False
9.    Sack
10.   False
11.   Ribbon
12.   True
13.   D
14.   A Christmas tree
15.   False, they were made from glass

# Answers

## Quiz 17:
## Christmas Decoration

1. Angel
2. Four
3. True
4. A sweet
5. Germany
6. Candles
7. False, they contained sweets
8. A piñata
9. Star
10. Norway
11. Red and white
12. Silver
13. Advent candles
14. A gingerbread house
15. Red

# Answers

## Quiz 17:
## Christmas Decoration

1. *El caganer*
2. A straw goat in Gävle
3. Dresden
4. Dala
5. Straw
6. Lanterns
7. Pōhutukawa
8. A nisse
9. Pineapple
10. When you can see the first star in the sky
11. Shoes
12. Tealight
13. The nativity scene
14. Straw
15. Rockerfeller Center

## Quiz 18:
## Christmas Trivia

1.  Jesus Christ

2.  D

3.  Spanish

4.  False, the first recorded Christmas is thought
    to be in 336 AD during the Roman Empire

5.  Gabriel

6.  French

7.  25 December

8.  Boxing Day

9.  Christmas Eve

10. B

11. False, Good Friday comes before Easter

12. D

13. Joseph

14. B

15. True

## Quiz 18:
## Christmas Trivia

1. *Natale*
2. Advent
3. C
4. False, it is the winter solstice
5. C
6. Yule log
7. A candle and an orange
8. Nativity
9. Parliament
10. False, it is a federal holiday
11. B
12. Gingerbread Man
13. False, some Orthodox churches celebrate around 7 January
14. B
15. A Christmas box

# Answers

## Quiz 18:
## Christmas Trivia

1. Epiphany

2. Shepherds

3. Boston

4. Russia

5. From east to west

6. 1843

7. Chris Rea

8. Germany

9. Orange

10. The eleventh Day of Christmas

11. The poem "Twas the Night Before Christmas'

12. Thanksgiving

13. Christmas Tree

14. 7 January

15. *Guinness World Records*

# Answers

## Quiz 19:
## General Knowledge

1.     C
2.     St. Nicholas
3.     Shaun the Sheep
4.     C
5.     False
6.     Top
7.     *Boots*
8.     80
9.     Olaf
10.    *Midwife*
11.    Their flocks (Sheep)
12.    On the shelf
13.    France or Belgium
14.    False, it wasn't until around the 1920s Father Christmas was consistently dressed in red
15.    Hogwarts

# Answers

## Quiz 19:
## General Knowledge

1.   *Single*

2.   Jacob Marley

3.   D

4.   William the Conqueror

5.   Birthdays on 25 December

6.   True

7.   Soldier

8.   Lord Mayor of London

9.   *Death in Paradise*

10.  *A Charlie Brown Christmas*

11.  Rejoice

12.  USA

13.  2012

14.  True

15.  New Year's Day

# Answers

## Quiz 19:
## General Knowledge

1. An elf
2. Fan Scrooge
3. Christmas Day
4. The Delaware River
5. Birthdays on 26 December
6. *The Nutcracker and the Mouse King*
7. 822 homes per second
8. Widow Twankey
9. Mackenzie Crook
10. *Klaus*
11. $H_2O$
12. Carol Aebersold and Chanda Bell
13. Hawaii
14. 'Christmas Man'
15. *The Darling Buds of May*

# Answers

## Quiz 20:
## Christmas Animations

1. *The Polar Express*
2. Malcolm Claus
3. *The Grinch*
4. *Guardians*
5. *Frozen 2*
6. Jesper Johansen
7. D
8. Olaf
9. Frosty the Snowman
10. *Father Christmas* and *Father Christmas Goes on Holiday*
11. Halloween
12. Rudolph
13. Scrooge McDuck
14. False, it is called *The Elf on the Shelf: An Elf's Story*
15. Grand Pabbie

## Quiz 20:
## Christmas Animations

1. S-1
2. *The Polar Express*
3. Benedict Cumberbatch
4. Jack Frost
5. D
6. 6,000
7. A Who-Man
8. Channel 4
9. 1969
10. France
11. Halloween Town
12. False, there was a book and a song featuring Rudolph before the animation
13. Mickey Mouse
14. A reindeer
15. Gin, Hana, Miyuki

# Answers

## Quiz 20:
## Christmas Animations

1. Pharrell Williams

2. Nicholas St. North

3. February

4. Ellingboes and Krums

5. Gillian Anderson

6. *When the Wind Blows*

7. Professor Hinkle

8. *Duck the Halls: A Mickey Mouse Christmas Special*

9. In the garbage

10. Pumpkin King of Halloween Town

11. Donner

12. Goofy

13. Charlie Brown (*A Charlie Brown Christmas*)

14. *Mickey's Twice Upon A Christmas*

15. Best Animated Feature and Best Original Song

# Answers

## Quiz 21:
## Christmas Songs

1.  Everyday
2.  False, it was number one in the USA in 2019, 2020 and 2021
3.  Band Aid
4.  The Darkness
5.  'Last Christmas'
6.  New York
7.  True
8.  'Don't Stop Me Eatin''
9.  A snowman
10. Jolly
11. John Lennon and Yoko Ono
12. Spanish
13. 'Santa Tell Me'
14. D
15. Cliff Richard

# Answers

## Quiz 21:
## Christmas Songs

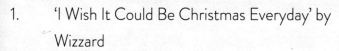

1. 'I Wish It Could Be Christmas Everyday' by Wizzard

2. *Merry Christmas*

3. Bob Geldof and Midge Ure

4. 'Mad World' by Michael Andrews and Gary Jules

5. True

6. Ewan MacColl

7. 'Bohemian Rhapsody' by Queen

8. False, it was number three

9. 'Merry Christmas' by Ed Sheeran and Elton John

10. Santa Claus

11. 'Mistletoe'

12. True

13. 'Own It' by Stormzy featuring Ed Sheeran and Burna Boy

14. Big Shaq

15. Elvis Presley

## Quiz 21:
## Christmas Songs

1. 1987

2. 2019

3. Nigel Planer as his character Neil Pye

4. Justin Hawkins

5. 'Do They Know It's Christmas?' by Band Aid

6. The NYPD don't have a choir

7. 'Girls' School'

8. Six

9. Mark Hoyle

10. *Meet Me In St. Louis*

11. 1958

12. Alexandra Burke (number one) and Jeff Buckley (number two)

13. Three ('Own It', 'Audacity', 'Lessons')

14. 'Too Much'

15. 'Hallelujah'

## Quiz 22:
## Christmas Traditions

1.    A
2.    24
3.    False but it is popular!
4.    Baby Jesus
5.    Eat it – it's yule log
6.    A Christmas jumper
7.    40 days
8.    Under the Christmas tree
9.    False, muktuk is a traditional food of whale skin and blubber
10.   Ice skating
11.   B
12.   False
13.   A
14.   In their shoes
15.   Cod

## Quiz 22:
## Christmas Traditions

1. C
2. True
3. A Christmas fruit cake
4. Christmas carols
5. A shoe
6. D
7. The Netherlands
8. At midnight on New Year's Eve
9. True
10. Portuguese
11. Gingerbread
12. Greenland
13. His sack (before taking them to Spain!)
14. Pie Face
15. 1988

# Answers

## Quiz 22:
## Christmas Traditions

1. Christmas Eve
2. A horse figure carried door to door by wassail-singing groups
3. The spirit of dead ancestors
4. Apple
5. Red
6. *Svyatki*
7. Pickle
8. 12
9. 13
10. Souls of the dead
11. Queen Victoria
12. Cookies
13. Montgomery Ward
14. Radishes
15. Bread

# Answers

## Quiz 23:
## Nativity

1. Nazareth
2. False, he was a carpenter
3. Mary and Joseph's journey to Bethlehem
4. C
5. There was no room
6. Shepherds
7. Gold, frankincense, myrrh
8. On a donkey
9. A manger
10. False
11. Martin Freeman
12. *The Star*
13. False
14. Drummer
15. Donkey, ox, sheep or camel

# Answers

## Quiz 23:
## Nativity

1.  A

2.  Three Magi or Kings

3.  Dusty

4.  A feeding trough for animals

5.  Death

6.  There was a census

7.  Lobster

8.  *Nativity 2: Danger in the Manger*

9.  *Story*

10. True, in *The Star*

11. Ben-Hur

12. Ricky Tomlinson

13. *Monty Python's The Life of Brian*

14. Greggs

15. David Bowie

# Answers

## Quiz 23:
## Nativity

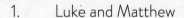

1. Luke and Matthew

2. Herod the Great

3. The Holy Spirit

4. 1,000 years

5. The Roman Catholic Church

6. No animals are mentioned

7. *Nativity 3: Dude, Where's My Donkey?*

8. *Nativity 4: Nativity Rocks!*

9. Palestine

10. King Herod

11. Simon of Cyrene

12. It doesn't specify

13. Church of the Nativity

14. Ashley Blake

15. Max von Sydow

## Quiz 24:
## Christmas Sport

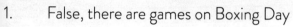

1. False, there are games on Boxing Day
2. B
3. D
4. Australia
5. Aaron Ramsey
6. 1914
7. False, NFL games are played on Christmas Day some years
8. Kamara
9. Jesus
10. B
11. False, they began in 1947
12. D
13. True
14. True

## Quiz 24:
## Christmas Sport

1.   D
2.   1925
3.   C
4.   Alastair Cook
5.   Pheasant shoot
6.   Australia
7.   Jamaica
8.   Brian Clough
9.   It was the first Football League starting line-up to contain no British players
10.  No man's land
11.  Michael Jordan
12.  1951
13.  Gary McAllister
14.  Big Air (freestyle skiing)
15.  False, it was until 1925

## Quiz 24:
## Christmas Sport

1. 1965

2. Northern Ireland

3. King George VI Chase

4. 2010

5. Sweden

6. Archery

7. More than 53,000

8. Colin Cowdrey

9. Australia and Sweden

10. The Hawthorns, West Bromwich Albion

11. Autumn Nations Cup

12. 1971

13. It was the longest game in NFL history at 82 minutes and 40 seconds

14. Boxing

15. Ghost to the Post

## Quiz 25:
## General Knowledge

1. Pigs in blankets

2. Tiny Tim

3. Robin

4. False, *Jack and the Beanstalk*

5. White

6. Eight

7. Greendale

8. False

9. Candy cane

10. D

11. Frankincense

12. True

13. Red

14. Button

15. Boo or hiss

# Answers

## Quiz 25:
## General Knowledge

1. Bacon

2. False, it was invented in Germany

3. *Cinderella*

4. Freddo

5. Whoville

6. 'White Christmas' by Bing Crosby

7. Christmas Day

8. Krampus

9. Brandy

10. *The Christmas Chronicles* and *The Christmas Chronicles 2*

11. Godric's Hollow

12. 26 December

13. Cupid

14. Marzipan

15. C

## Quiz 25:
## General Knowledge

1. 1610
2. It is steamed
3. Postmen
4. A wooden log
5. Donner and Blitzen
6. Four: Christmas Past, Christmas Present, Christmas Yet to Come, Jacob Marley's Ghost
7. Hen
8. Yule Lads (Jólasveinar)
9. 25 December
10. Clove
11. 'Rudolph the Red Nosed Reindeer' (1949), 'Frosty the Snowman' (1950)
12. Kwanzaa
13. *In God We Trust, All Others Pay Cash* by Jean Shepherd
14. Goats
15. Capricorn

## Quiz 26:
## Christmas Sweets

1. Tray

2. Celebrations

3. Caramel and a hazelnut

4. False

5. B

6. Triangle

7. True

8. Milky Bar

9. Eclair

10. No, it is only toffee

11. A

12. Terry's

13. Creme Egg Twisted

14. False

15. False

# Answers

## Quiz 26:
## Christmas Sweets

1.  Ferrero Rocher
2.  Cadbury Milk Tray
3.  C
4.  Mackintosh
5.  The Purple One
6.  Malteser Teasers
7.  The Green Triangle
8.  Caramel
9.  Round
10. False, there is a White Raspberry
11. Nine
12. You
13. 1938
14. False, it was called Peanut Cracknell
15. Blue

## Quiz 26:
## Christmas Sweets

1.  Cath Kidston

2.  J. M. Barrie

3.  Hazel in Caramel

4.  Brazilian

5.  'All the Fun of the Share'

6.  1990s

7.  1997

8.  Rowntree

9.  Dinky Decker

10. 1958

11. Dairy Milk (1905), Bournville (1908)

12. 1938

13. Halifax

14. They have all previously been included in the Heroes selection box

15. 1936

# Answers

## Quiz 27:
## Christmas Characters

1. Janet and Allan Ahlberg

2. Elves

3. False, the Snowman flies

4. Arthur Claus

5. D

6. The Conductor

7. Green

8. True

9. *The Snowman and the Snowdog*

10. False, it is Cindy Lou Who

11. C

12. White

13. Dur Pig (or DP)

14. A polar bear

15. Amelia Wishart

# Answers

## Quiz 27:
## Christmas Characters

1. Skellington
2. False, it is black and white
3. Mr Poppy
4. Alan Rickman
5. *Kranks*
6. Gizmo
7. Emma Thompson
8. *Rudolph the Red-Nosed Reindeer*
9. Uncle Billy
10. Five
11. Fred
12. *Magic*
13. Steven Claus
14. *The Christmas Pine*
15. Sally Brown

## Quiz 27:
## Christmas Characters

1. *The Chimes*
2. 1947 and 1994
3. Pete, Janie, Zuzu and Tommy
4. Cousin Eddie
5. Natalie Wood
6. *The Year Without Santa Claus*
7. Martha Cratchit
8. Willie T. Soke
9. Albert Finney
10. Bill Murray
11. Alastair Sim
12. Michael Caine
13. George C. Scott
14. Eight
15. Catherine O'Hara

## Quiz 28:
## Christmas Mix

1. A jumper and fudge
2. Marshmallow
3. *Pooped*
4. A
5. *Cinderella*
6. Dancer, Dasher, Donner
7. Bells
8. Jack
9. C
10. D
11. *The 12 Days of Christmas*
12. True
13. Quality Street
14. *Home Alone*
15. False

# Answers

## Quiz 28:
## Christmas Mix

1. Blue ('Blue Christmas')

2. Four

3. Christmas

4. Jennifer Aniston

5. Clarence Odbody

6. David Tennant

7. Christmas Day

8. D

9. Max

10. *Moby Dick*

11. Emma Thompson

12. 'Treat every day like Christmas'

13. Nine years

14. 'Jingle Bell Rock'

15. Dolly Parton

## Quiz 28:
## Christmas Mix

1. Matthew Crawley

2. Bob Dylan

3. 2006

4. Kilted soldiers

5. Blue

6. 'Let it Snow, Let it Snow, Let it Snow'

7. 1949

8. Forest Whitaker

9. 2021

10. The Soviet Union

11. 'Santa's Super Sleigh'

12. Frode Fjellheim

13. Gobbler

14. Belle

15. Harry Lyme and Marv Murchins

## Quiz 29:
## Christmas in the British Isles

1. D
2. True
3. Christmas Day
4. False, it is pre-recorded
5. D
6. *Lake*
7. 25 December and 26 December
8. C
9. They have had the same number – three
10. False, it's a swim
11. A fifty pence piece
12. Sweets
13. D (she is known as Nana Baubles)
14. Boxing Day sales
15. A cow

## Quiz 29:
## Christmas in the British Isles

1.   B
2.   Twelfth Cake (or Twelfth Night Cake)
3.   July
4.   False, it is called the Wassail bowl
5.   1981
6.   Scotland
7.   Toffee – it translates to Toffee Evening
8.   None
9.   Bells, for a tradition known as the Devil's Knell
10.  Wales
11.  A family eating a Christmas meal
12.  1984
13.  True
14.  25 December 1977
15.  Northern Ireland

# Answers

## Quiz 29:
## Christmas in the British Isles

1.  The Stone of Scone
2.  Pilchards (sardines)
3.  2020
4.  Rhymes
5.  1974
6.  Sheffield Carols
7.  Cornwall
8.  5 km (3.1 miles)
9.  *Siôn Corn*
10. A drink
11. To signal to Mary and Joseph they were welcome
12. Burning whisky barrels
13. Advent
14. The Purple One
15. Coconut Eclair

# Answers

## Quiz 30: Yuletide

1. Mistletoe
2. False
3. B
4. The Sun
5. False, singing was common
6. Yule log
7. A
8. Winter solstice
9. False, it evolved from Old English
10. D
11. Eat, it's a Scandinavian feast
12. A drink, it's a type of mulled wine popular in Victorian England
13. Mince
14. False
15. A

# Answers

## Quiz 30: Yuletide

1. A
2. Druid
3. Odin
4. False, they would visit orchards
5. Eggnog
6. False, it often falls on 21 December
7. Eight
8. Yule log
9. C
10. Mulled wine
11. The Sun
12. Elves
13. Green
14. D, the others are drinks
15. 12 days

## Quiz 30:
## Yuletide

1. Saturnalia

2. Bacchus

3. A wassail bowl

4. Christmas

5. Sleipnir

6. India

7. Misrule

8. Balder (Baldr)

9. Latin, from *solstitium*

10. Wassail

11. Mistletoe

12. Nine hours

13. 336 AD

14. Carol (or carole)

15. Twelfth Night

## Quiz 31:
## General Knowledge

1. Sven

2. *Whittington*

3. *The Polar Express*: Hero Boy, Father, Conductor, Hobo, Scrooge puppet, Santa Claus

4. Tiny Tim

5. Myrrh

6. Dream

7. Arendelle

8. The Triwizard Tournament

9. B

10. Mr. Magoo

11. World

12. Saint Nicholas

13. Green

14. In a pear tree

15. False, Creme Egg Twisted is in Cadbury Heroes

## Quiz 31:
## General Knowledge

1. True

2. Presents

3. David Suchet

4. *Christmas*

5. *The Office*

6. Will Smith

7. Dave Coaches

8. False, he voices Don Juan Diego in *Jingle Jangle*

9. The Northuldra

10. Dr Leonardo

11. Marley

12. Santa hats

13. Nine

14. She runs a launderette

15. False, he's in *Home Alone 2*

## Quiz 31:
## General Knowledge

1.     A columnist for the *Daily Telegraph*

2.     Emilia Clarke

3.     Jangles and Things

4.     Brad and Kate

5.     Best Original Score and Best Original Song

6.     *Love's Labour Lost* and *Taming of the Shrew*

7.     Mr Fezziwig

8.     Beethoven's Ninth Symphony

9.     1647

10.     *Sleeping Beauty*

11.     Sky Cinema

12.     Mince pies

13.     2020

14.     Grandfather Christmas

15.     His nephew, Fred

## Quiz 32:
## Movie Favourites: *Home Alone*

1. Chicago
2. Culkin
3. Buzz
4. For his family to disappear
5. New York
6. C
7. Miami
8. Pigeons
9. False
10. 10 years old
11. B
12. False, it was a made-for-television film
13. Kieran Culkin
14. *Home Sweet Home Alone*
15. One year

## Quiz 32:
## Movie Favourites: *Love Actually*

1.  Heathrow Airport
2.  Joe
3.  'All You Need Is Love'
4.  His brother
5.  A heart
6.  A Joni Mitchell CD
7.  Billy Bob Thornton appears in both films
8.  Joanna
9.  Claudia Schiffer
10. Milwaukee
11. John and Judy
12. Michael
13. Karl
14. Rufus
15. Richard Curtis

## Quiz 32:
## Movie Favourites: *Love Actually*

1.   Billy Mack and Joe
2.   Stacey, Jeannie and Carol-Anne
3.   Richard Curtis
4.   'Jump'
5.   In a pond
6.   9/11
7.   2003
8.   Saab
9.   'I said I'm not hungry'
10.  Ugliest man
11.  A scarf
12.  Frances de la Tour
13.  Stand-ins for movie actors
14.  Jeanne Moreau
15.  Shepperton Studios

## Quiz 33:
## Tick Tock

1. Nine
2. Mince pies
3. C
4. *Encanto*
5. White and red
6. White
7. A carrot
8. Six
9. A
10. An advent calendar
11. Brussels sprouts
12. *Snow White and the Seven Dwarfs*
13. C
14. False
15. Three

## Quiz 33:
## Tick Tock

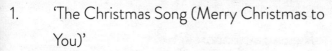

1. 'The Christmas Song (Merry Christmas to You)'
2. Marzipan
3. 'All I Want For Christmas (Is My Two Front Teeth)'
4. *Aladdin*
5. Two
6. Dr Christmas Jones
7. 'I'm Walking Backwards for Christmas'
8. Tom Conti
9. Arnold Schwarzenegger
10. Sandringham
11. Westlife
12. Paul Young
13. Hulk Hogan
14. Peru
15. 'You Send Me' by Aretha Franklin

## Quiz 33:
## Tick Tock

1. Donald Duck
2. Richard Attenborough
3. 'All I Want For Christmas Is A Dukla Prague Away Kit'
4. Scotland (1640), England (1647)
5. *The Sword in the Stone*
6. Mistletoe
7. Bohemia
8. Turbo Man
9. *The Adventure of the Blue Carbuncle*
10. Sweden
11. '¡Happy Birthday Guadalupe!'
12. P.D. James
13. 1966
14. *Shatner Claus*
15. *The Pickwick Papers*

## Quiz 34:
## Happy New Year

1.   New Year's Eve

2.   January

3.   Fireworks

4.   Back door

5.   'Auld Lang Syne'

6.   True

7.   Big Ben

8.   D

9.   True

10.  B

11.  False

12.  Coal

13.  Go for a swim

14.  False

15.  Times Square

# Answers

## Quiz 34:
## Happy New Year

1.      B
2.      12
3.      Denmark
4.      First footing
5.      B
6.      Fireballs
7.      Italy
8.      1 January and 2 January
9.      A bear
10.     A ball
11.     Julian calendar
12.     They were born on 1 January
13.     The Millennium Bug or Y2K Bug
14.     Robert Burns
15.     Tiger

## Quiz 34:
## Happy New Year

1. B
2. Welsh
3. Old long since
4. Steak pie
5. B
6. Tall and dark-haired
7. Onions
8. Lead
9. The Netherlands
10. A suitcase
11. Gregorian calendar
12. *The Times*
13. The European Economic Community (EEC)
14. The Rose Bowl Game
15. Kiribati (parts of it)

# Notes

# Notes

# Notes

# Notes

# Notes

# Notes